BLACK CHRISTIANS AND
WHITE MISSIONARIES

BLACK CHRISTIANS
AND
WHITE MISSIONARIES

RICHARD GRAY

YALE UNIVERSITY PRESS
NEW HAVEN AND LONDON 1990

To Gabriella,

my wife and fellow pilgrim

78692229

Set in Linotron Bembo by Excel Typesetters Co., Hong Kong
Printed in Great Britain by

Library of Congress Cataloging-in-Publication Data

Gray, Richard, 1929–
  Black Christians and White missionaries/by Richard Gray.
    ‌ cm.
  Includes bibliographical references and index.
  ISBN 0-300-04910-2
  1. Missions – Africa, Sub-Saharan.   2. Africa, Sub-Saharan –
Religion.   I. Title.
BV3520.G72   1991
276.7 – dc20   90-40030
                                                                     CIP

Printed in Great Britain by Bell and Bain Ltd., Glasgow

Contents

CONTENTS

Preface

These two groups of essays are the result of rather different forms of historical investigation. The first group consists of fairly recent work based largely on research in Rome into the sources relating to sub-Saharan Africa in the seventeenth century. It is a task which I hope to pursue in the years ahead, when it may become possible to merge these first snapshots into a more comprehensive, coherent account. The second group, dealing with the modern period, consists of reflections derived largely from reading the research and writing of other scholars, as I have been able to study various aspects of Christianity in Africa with a succession of undergraduate and postgraduate students at the School of Oriental and African Studies. Nearly all the essays were first discussed at seminars at SOAS and elsewhere in Britain, Africa, Jerusalem, Rome and Harvard. I hope that participants on these occasions will see where I have benefited from their comments and will forgive me where I have failed to do so. To all of them I offer my very grateful thanks, but especially to Humphrey Fisher. Many of my insights derive from, or were transformed and sharpened by, the courses we have run together. His wide knowledge of the history of Islam in sub-Saharan Africa has illuminated that of Christianity; his generous, detailed critical comments on our scripts have saved me and many a student from innumerable errors and infelicities; while his own religious commitment has often revealed to us the deeper challenges of a Christian discipleship.

My thanks are also due in the first place to Father Albert Plangger, the Director of Mambo Press in Zimbabwe, who first suggested to me the possibility of such a collection of

essays. I feel greatly honoured to be thus associated, in however minor a way, with the work of this Press. During the
darkest days of the UDI regime the Mambo Press placed
itself unreservedly in the service of justice and liberation and
it continues to serve these objectives in a country to which
my wife and I are very deeply attached. Secondly I would
like to thank Robert Baldock, his readers and assistants at
Yale University Press for their help in turning these essays
into a book. Grateful acknowledgements are also due to the
following publishers for permission to reprint work which
has appeared elsewhere: The Rector of the Istituto Univer-
sitario Orientale, Naples, for chapter 2; the International
African Institute, London, for chapter 3; Sage Publications
Inc., The Royal African Society, London, and Longmans
Group Ltd for material appearing in chapter 4. Chapter 1 is
reprinted with the permission of The Past and Present
Society (from *Past and Present: A Journal of Historical Studies*,
no. 115 (May 1987), pp. 52–68), which retains world
copyright.

PART ONE

African Cosmologies and First Appropriations of Christianity

The underlying theme of this book is the distinction between the concepts and practices of Christianity, as brought to sub-Saharan Africa by European and North American missionaries, and the ways in which this Christianity has been appropriated by Black Africans and their diaspora descendants. The tensions inherent in this contrast have often disturbed, alarmed and depressed those who carried the faith to Africa. Yet, since Christianity aspires to the status of a universal religion, there should be nothing surprising about this distinction. Inevitably the Gospel carries implications which transcend the understanding of those who proclaim it. Christian scriptures and sacraments have, as it were, escaped from the hands and minds of those who brought them, and have spoken directly to the various and very differing needs of Africans. Even within the same society, the transmission of the faith across generations presents startling difficulties; when it is transmitted across continents and cultures, it sometimes appears at first sight to be almost unrecognizable.

In this book, the focus is not on some of the stranger manifestations of these transformations. There is relatively little reference to the visions induced by the combination of Christianity, Fang culture and the drug Eboga, or to the cries and shakings of the wilder forms of spirit possession.[1] Rather it seeks to explore, mainly within the records of the mission-connected churches, some of the less dramatic, yet nevertheless basic, differences of emphasis which have distinguished the Christianity of some Africans and of their descendants in the diaspora.

Some of the dynamics which have helped to shape African appropriations of Christianity stem from the roles played by religion in pre-Christian African societies. When European missionaries first went to tropical Africa, it was assumed that Black Africans had no religion, no complex, satisfying views of the world, of human destiny and of supernatural powers. Even Erasmus, with his more open and cultured approach, asked in 1534: "In Africa what have we? There are surely in these vast tracts barbarous and simple tribes who could easily be attracted to Christ if we sent men among them to sow the good seed."[2] African religions, however, were by no means simple to understand. There was an immense variety of religious beliefs and practices across the continent, and, as in most areas before the Age of Enlightenment, beliefs about human relationships with supernatural powers were at the heart of much African social and political thought.

Religion could legitimate the status quo. Ancestors, the living dead who had power to influence the fate and future of their descendants, were crucial to many family or kinship systems, which were the basic networks of most African societies. Respect for the ancestors, shown in prayer, libation and sacrifice, legitimated at homestead and village level the practical control of the lineage's resources by its elders. Such respect also reinforced the dependence of strangers, slaves or clients on a lineage. In the case of royal ancestors, their influence transcended kinship relationships to embrace all loyal subjects of a kingdom.

A state and a kingdom, however, mobilized or incorporated not merely ancestral powers but also many other supernatural forces. Perhaps the most ancient were those intimately linked to a specific locality: a cave, a mountain peak, a massive venerable tree, a spring or a stretch of water. The spirits associated with these places were often the first supernatural forces to cut across kinship links.[3] The priests of these spirits or divinities could challenge or supplement the dictates of the ancestors. These shrines tended however to remain stubbornly indentified with particular, provincial loyalties. Sometimes they could become articulated into a cult stretching across a wide region, embracing a number of similar local priesthoods. But more often a nascent power which wished to centralize its authority would have to overcome or transcend such priesthoods, relegating them to minor, marginal significance. In this process, the mobility of a spirit and its shrine was often a crucial factor. Royal emblems, such as golden stools, copper spears, wrought-iron double bells or other impressive creations of African sculpture and craftsmanship, assumed a critical significance: they could become the focus of the hopes and fears of everyone associated with the kingdom. The great state occasions were essentially religious rituals. People forgot for a time the drudgery of the fields or the dangers of the hunt, and they united with their rulers in ceremonies of renewal and recreation. The rhythm of life was regularly moulded and given meaning by the demands, sometimes joyful, sometimes fearful, of dance, ritual and sacrifice.[4] Royal power could mightily protect from all forms of evil, even those which enlightened philosophers in other societies would characterize as mere misfortune.

Supernatural powers did not, however, merely legitimate African political systems. The gods did not automatically support the rule of kings or elders. As elsewhere, religion possessed a critical, prophetic dimension. A king, just as much as his subjects, could be confined by taboo. His power and efficacy depended on the assistance of many ritual experts. His initiation or coronation involved a host of functionaries; without their participation, its validity was impaired or negated. His insignia clearly indicated his power and status to the populace. They alone set him apart; without them, he could not perform his role. Yet insignia, together with royal charms and the kingdom's shrines, were jealously guarded by their custodians. If religion sustained the ruler, it also imposed rigid limits to the royal will; the ruler found himself dependent on others, entrapped and hedged around by an endless array of obligations and taboos.

This dependence of rulers on custom and on ritual experts was merely one way in which religion could limit, confront and challenge political power. Generally this critical function was confined to the correction of sporadic, specific abuses. It constrained the corrupting influences of power. It mobilized and legitimated an opposition. Religion, however, also had a prophetic potential; it could express a far more radical critique. It could supply the weapons and provide the base from which an attack could be launched against the holders of power. A rebellion could be initiated under a religious banner. Occasionally religion could legitimate a revolution, a full-scale attempt to transform the whole political system.

Rebellions and revolutions are difficult to discern in the records of oral tradition, on which we depend for so much of our knowledge of pre-colonial Africa. Traditions often provided the charter or justification for a political order, so even if the system had originated in revolution, its origins might soon become clothed in respectability, and successful rebellions could be glossed over with rapidity. This process was assisted by the ability of African indigenous religions to assimilate new insights and fresh rituals. The approach of most Africans to supernatural powers was pragmatic and experimental. As a result, shrines, cults, ritual practices and religious beliefs could accumulate to form a palimpsest, a record of ideological change and development. Among the Mbundu in Angola, Miller has clearly identified such a sequence of religious symbols. It culminates with the Imbangala, who swept through West Central Africa in the seventeenth century and provide a dramatic example of the revolutionary political potential of religious innovation. Miller describes how the power of the Imbangala stemmed originally from the fusion of two very different religious institutions. One was a royal title, the *kinguri*, which was linked to a set of powerful symbols and charms. This title moved westwards from the Lunda area deep in what is now Zaïre, probably in the late sixteenth century, founding a variety of political units until the Imbangala, a heterogeneous band of people, came under its influence. The Imbangala joined this source of power to that of a secret society, the *kilombo*, which had previously existed among the Ovimbundu in southern Angola. Entry to the *kilombo*, as it was developed by the Imbangala, involved dramatic initiation rituals which liberated its members from the power of all other supernatural sanctions. One of the central features of this cult was reputed to involve the sacrifice of a child born of an incestuous union, an act which symbolized the abolition of lineages or "the denial of the social significance of a physical birth".[5]

A reductionist, determined to deny any creative significance to religious innovations, might conceivably argue that
the beliefs and sanctions connected with the Imbangala rituals
were merely an *ex post facto* elaboration, devised to explain
and legitimate the military impact of a band of mercenary
slavers. The religious factor had not created the Imbangala
revolution; it had merely sanctified it. Such an interpretation,
however, would overlook one of the deepest and most
enduring desires of all African societies: the anxiety to eliminate evil.

Evil was experienced as that which destroyed life, health,
strength, fertility and prosperity. Of course Africans recognized the immediate causes of death, but for them the
crucial task was to look behind these phenomena to discover
the ultimate, determining causes. African cosmologies had
little if any room for the secularized concept of pure chance
or misfortune. They assumed that if supernatural evil were
absent, all would be well and good. The dualism so deeply
rooted in Judaeo-Christian thought was seldom present.
Supernatural forces were not patterned on the dichotomy of
God and the Devil. Evil, in the sense of suffering, was not
generally accepted as an inescapable part of human life. Evil
entered societies from various sources. It was sometimes
produced by a failure to respect the ancestors or other supernatural forces, by a neglect of rituals due to them, or by the
breaking – intentional or unintentional – of their prohibi-
tions. These failures could generally be countered by an
appropriate sacrifice or ritual, but there were occasions when
jealousy, hatred, envy and malice could seize hold of an
individual and even take complete possession, transforming
the person into a witch. This evil of sorcery, witchcraft and
the misuse of spiritual power was felt to pose the greatest
threat to many African peoples, so the political and religious
institutions of many African societies were designed to
counteract its influence. Elders, diviners and rulers were all
expected to provide protection against this evil. The failings
of humanity and the incidence of misfortune combined,
however, to ensure that the experience of evil was omnipres-
ent. At times of prolonged crisis, the burden of evil could
become almost unbearable. A fresh mode of supernatural

assistance, bringing with it the hope of a return to pristine order, was therefore a potential challenge to a political system which had, in various ways, manifestly failed to protect its members. Elders and rulers sought therefore to assimilate and accommodate such novel sources of power. But if they failed, initiation into the *kilombo*, or any other cult which proclaimed salvation or the power to eradicate evil, could provide the opportunity for radical political change, for a prophetic revolution.

These fundamental assumptions about the nature of the world and the place of human beings within it have profoundly influenced the development of African Christianity. The new religion was often seen as a fresh source of supernatural power. It could enhance and support existing concepts and structures; it could challenge and endanger the status quo; it could help to bring liberation in various forms. The final chapter of this book examines how concepts of evil have evolved, but the interaction with other African religious practices and beliefs has also been of central significance for African Christianity. Whereas at first most missionaries assumed that they were committed to a frontal assault on what they saw as African superstitions, in the twentieth century some Western missionaries and many African theologians have come to regard indigenous religions, especially the widespread beliefs in God as Creator, as a wonderfully valid preparation for the Christian Gospel. Other African Christians have found in Christianity healing and even a home for the ancestors. The nature and heritage of African religious experiences go far to explain the distinctive contributions which Africans are bringing to the universal church.

The essays in Part I of this book explore some of the ways in which Africans had begun to appropriate Christianity at a time when the European missionaries with whom they were in contact shared many aspects of African cosmologies. Few if any white missionaries to Africa in the seventeenth century saw indigenous religions as a preparation for Christianity. Nevertheless they were in many respects far closer to Africans in their approach to the supernatural than were most of their successors in the nineteenth or twentieth centuries. For the Capuchins, who went to the kingdom of Kongo and who there entered into a more intimate relationship with Black Africans, and on a scale far greater than that achieved by any other missionaries prior to the nineteenth century, the supernatural intervened in human predicaments in many miraculous or nefarious ways. Much of the armoury which had previously been treasured by the Kongo in their conflict with maleficent spiritual forces was condemned by the missionaries. New ritual weapons were provided for the baptized and practising Christian communities. But for both Black and White Christians, the battle against the forces of evil involved much the same spectrum of human concerns and activities. Harvests, rainfall, defence against locusts and other predators, healing, victory and security were still dependent on ritual, practice and belief. Religion had yet to be marginalized as a separate component of life.

Yet despite, or perhaps because of, these profound cosmological similarities, Black Christians were already developing their own specific characteristics and emphases. One of the fascinating aspects of Lourenço da Silva, the principal figure in Chapter 1, is that he provides us with some rare insights into the world of the Luso-Brazilian slaves in the late seventeenth century. We know so little about him or that world of his, and it is difficult to be dogmatic concerning his appropriations of Christianity. Nevertheless the petitions he presented in Rome vividly demonstrate how the concepts of European Catholicism had been assimilated to meet the needs and demands of oppressed Blacks. The shrewd appeal to Iberian and Catholic prejudices, for instance against the Jews, is manifest, but beneath this there are ideas and sentiments which speak to the fundamentals of a universal Christianity. For Lourenço and his fellow Black Christians, the faith brought the hope of liberation, it demanded a commitment to the cause of the poor and the oppressed, and it involved an equality of treatment for "any and every Christian". Here, in one of the earliest statements still extant of Black slaves, we find already clearly enunciated the basic characteristics of what in the twentieth century would be recognized as Black Theology.

These petitions, and the very presence of Lourenço in Rome, opened the eyes of the Cardinals of Propaganda Fide,

the Congregation established by the pope in 1622 to super-
vise Catholic missionary activity. Their attention was suddenly directed to a fresh understanding of the implications of
their faith. The whole episode illustrates the development of
a moral, prophetic viewpoint. The Curia was prompted to
reassess its attitude to a social and economic evil which by the
late seventeenth century was assuming horrific proportions.
Lourenço's petitions were narrowly focused on the plight of
baptized slaves. His concerns were deepened and widened by
the formulations of the Capuchins, whose understanding of
their Order's option for poverty had been sharpened by their
own first-hand knowledge of the Atlantic system in Cuba
and elsewhere. The intervention of this Black Christian,
supported by these missionaries, resulted in the Curia seeing
for the first time the consequences of the slave trade in its
wider, human dimensions. The horizons of Christendom
were enlarged; the church's notion of evil was extended. But
this advance was only for a moment. The practical consequences of Lourenço's mission were pitifully meagre, and
Chapter 2, with its examination of a mistranslated phrase in
the book by Fra Girolamo Merolla da Sorrento, explores one
reason why this was so.

Fra Girolamo should be remembered, however, not so
much for the misleading interpretation of Propaganda's
instruction concerning the slave trade, as for his account of
the Christianity practised by the ruling elite and by the
humbler people in Soyo, a province of the kingdom of
Kongo. Like the other Capuchin missionaries who worked
in Kongo and Angola in the seventeenth century, Fra Girolamo saw much to criticize, much that seemed to him contrary to Christian doctrine and ethics in the lives of baptized
Soyo Christians. Some other Capuchin accounts are indeed
almost unrelievedly critical and pessimistic. With other
Western missionaries, both then and later, some Capuchins
failed to appreciate the extent to which their own understanding of Christianity had been moulded and distorted
by their culture and upbringing. Fra Girolamo, however,
obviously established a close rapport with several of these
African Christians. He understood something of their mode
of religious interaction and development, and his evidence

provided the starting point for a reassessment, in Chapter 3, of the nature of the beliefs and practices of these Black Christians in this early period.

Far from being a pale and weak imitation of European religion, a fragile exotic plant, as some writers suggest, Christianity in late seventeenth-century Soyo was fast becoming a dominant force which legitimated political authority. Christian rituals were supplanting traditional modes of protecting the ruler and the state in peace and in war. Intimate involvement as youths in the service of the mission played a major role in selecting and forming the ruling elite. Membership of the religious confraternities, with their rigid ethical codes and disciplined rituals, had become prerequisites for political promotion. This training and attachment had resulted in many of the ruling elite developing an extraordinary, deep identification with Christianity. It even involved their at least nominal acceptance of canon law marriage.

Yet the process of conversion did not depend merely on a simple acceptance of missionary precepts and discipline. The confraternities, the spearhead and focus of this religious change, combined strict ecclesiastical ethics with indigenous concepts of purification and healing. Their members, especially perhaps those less educated, found in their activities salvation from fears of witchcraft and other forms of evil. The widespread demand for baptism and the willingness to come to the confessional probably answered similar needs among the wider populace. Within little more than a generation, the ancient, pervasive attention to and concern for the ancestors was becoming channelled into the church's commemoration of and prayers for the dead.

This appropriation of Christianity to meet the particular needs of Christians in Soyo was not without tension. Few of the people in Soyo deliberately sought a solution in syncretism, a purposeful attempt to create a distinct, new religious amalgam. Yet many sought to retain much of their former practices and beliefs. The distinction between the Black Christians and the White missionaries was marked. In the face of rigid missionary demands, the desire of Africans to preserve their cultural inheritance provoked anguish and conflict. A few of the more perceptive Capuchins were beginning to shed their Eurocentric prejudices and even to recognize some of the fundamental religious values of the people of Soyo. There was a fruitful interaction at certain levels, and the cumulative influence of a literate religious tradition was already clearly visible. Soyo was perhaps the only area in the early sub-Saharan mission field where Catholicism was extending roots of such depth and vigour, but even there, in the absence of a well-educated indigenous priesthood and laity, there was little prospect of theological dialogue and development in this brief, early period of close encounter.

CHAPTER 1

The Papacy and the Atlantic Slave Trade: Lourenço da Silva, the Capuchins and the Decisions of the Holy Office

Lourenço da Silva de Mendouça[1] was an extraordinary figure to arrive as an envoy at the papal Curia in the 1680s. Of Afro-Brazilian origin, he represented no powerful institution, temporal or religious. He came armed with some vague recommendations from Lisbon and Madrid; together with these, a scrap of paper alone contained a hint of his secret purpose. We do not know how he reached Rome, nor how long he stayed there. We know frustratingly little about his previous career, and nothing about his subsequent fortunes. Yet his visit and protests led the highest organs of the church to deliver a judgement on 20 March 1686 which is among the most notable statements on human rights ever to have been published by the papacy.

It has previously been assumed that the Catholic church, as an institution, played no part in challenging European attitudes concerning the Atlantic slave trade. In his erudite and witty survey of this theme, Charles Boxer concludes that the contribution of the papacy to the humanitarian attack on slavery "was precisely nil before the year 1839 – and very little between that date and 1888, when slavery was finally abolished in Brazil", though Boxer does draw attention to "a very few maverick individuals who *did* condemn the African slave trade as being inherently unjustifiable, unchristian and immoral".[2] It is significant that, just as Lourenço's first-hand testimony in Rome was needed to jolt the papacy into action, so these other individual Catholic writers based their condemnation not merely on abstract principles, but on their personal knowledge of the evils arising from the actual operation of the slave trade. Mercado, one of the first moralists to discuss at some length the ethics of this trade, described in detail some of the horrendous crimes being committed on the Guinea coast. He concluded that the slave trade, as practised there, was mortally sinful, since many of the Africans were enslaved by crime and violence.[3] Another prominent critic of the Atlantic slave trade was the Jesuit, Alonso de Sandoval, who suggested extensive reforms based on his long experience with African slaves at Cartagena in South America. These reforms, Boxer concludes, "were so far-reaching that, if implemented, they would in effect have made [the slave trade] quite impracticable and so resulted in its abandonment or abolition".[4] Yet, as a direct result of Lourenço's mission, the Holy Office approved a set of propositions which, had they been implemented, would have had precisely the same effect.

Lourenço da Silva himself claimed royal ancestry. The first petition which he presented to Innocent XI begins with the proud statement that he was of "the royal blood of the kings of Congo and Angola".[5] None of the other scanty evidence definitely confirms this claim; all we know with reasonable certainty is that he was a Mulatto, probably born in Brazil,[6] presumably of slave origins. Yet his claim is not impossible. Even before the battle of Ambuila, which in 1665 destroyed the central power of the kingdom of Kongo, succession to the throne there had often been disputed. It is therefore by no means unlikely that some of the royal contestants had been sold into slavery. Indeed "some eight or more years" before the battle of Ambuila, a Capuchin missionary had been given a young boy of noble birth, whom subsequently he had taken back to Italy.[7]

Lourenço's claim of royal connections, however remote they may have been, is also consistent with the fact that he was a recognized Black leader when he eventually emerged in Portugal. We do not know how or when he reached Lisbon, but on 15 February 1681 an affidavit signed by Gaspar da Costa de Mezquita, an apostolic notary in Lisbon, described how Lourenço was recognized as the "competent procurator of all the Mulattos throughout this kingdom, as in Castile and Brazil, so that he might obtain a papal brief concerning a certain matter for which they are petitioning".[8]

Over a year later, on 23 September 1682, "Don Lourenço", then resident at the court of Madrid, was formally appointed procurator of the Confraternity of Our Lady Star of the Negroes. In this office, he was empowered to establish branches of the confraternity "in any city, town or place whatsoever within the kingdoms of his majesty, as also throughout the whole of Christendom in any kingdom or dominion".[9]

In Kongo and Angola, and especially in Brazil and Portugal, lay confraternities or brotherhoods played an important role in the lives of Christians of African origin. Their activities and aspirations were an essential factor leading to Lourenço's mission to Rome. Modelled on the lay confraternities which have been termed "the most characteristic expressions of late medieval Christianity",[10] these Black confraternities served a variety of religious and social purposes. In both Portugal and Brazil, Blacks were able to participate in governing their own confraternities, for the crown saw these associations as a useful means of social control. Their constitutions and privileges were carefully recorded and jealously guarded. Participation in their governing councils conferred social prestige on a few Blacks and Mulattos, and for their members at large the confraternities acted as mutual aid societies. When funds permitted, members were assisted when they were sick or in prison. Membership entailed a wide range of religious obligations, including daily prayers and monthly confession and communion. Their regular activities were focused on their own chapels or, in the case of poorer groups, on the altar that they shared in a parish church or in the chapel of a more prosperous confraternity. At a local, interpersonal level, this formal worship provided a powerful focus for a common identity. Above all, members were assured of the last rites of the church and of a respectable burial, for all confraternities guaranteed the attendance of their members at the funeral of a fellow. Black confraternities were slower to develop in Brazil than in Portugal, but by the second half of the seventeenth century they were becoming significant there, and by the eighteenth century most towns in Brazil had a multiplicity of Black confraternities.[11]

Although the confraternities mainly voiced the concerns and furthered the interests of a small, elite minority, they also provided a model and rallying-point for less fortunate Blacks. By defending specifically Black and Mulatto causes, they proclaimed a measure of dignity, self-respect and hope for Blacks as a whole. As "the only form of communal life legally permitted" to slaves and freed Blacks in colonial Brazil, the confraternities offered a respectable alternative to the revolutionary *quilombos* or settlements formed by runaway slaves. To the Whites, they "represented moderation, authority and stability".[12]

In Africa itself, the confraternities played a significant role in the local response to the Capuchin mission in Kongo and Angola.[13] In Luanda, the Confraternity of Our Lady of the Rosary drew its membership from Blacks and slaves. In 1658, soon after its foundation, its members requested from Rome a formal recognition of its privileges. Their request illustrates how the members of these confraternities appropriated Christian values and applied them to the conditions in which they found themselves. The petitioners in Luanda sought to protect themselves against the pretensions of Whites "since," as they maintained, "in the service of God we must all be equal".[14] Across the Atlantic, in Bahia the Confraternity of Our Lady of the Rosary was at first limited to Blacks of Angolan origin and it became a recognized mouthpiece for Black rights.[15]

In Lisbon people of African descent had belonged to another Confraternity of Our Lady of the Rosary almost two centuries before Lourenço was recognized to be one of the leaders of the Mulattos there. In the sixteenth century the confraternity had flourished. It established branches in at least half a dozen other centres, held elaborate ceremonies and also sought to maintain the rights of free Blacks and of slaves seeking manumission.[16] Its rule and privileges were renewed by João IV in 1646 and were extended by Pedro II in 1688, for people of African descent were still a prominent feature of the Lisbon scene.[17] Almost certainly Lourenço was a leading member of this Lisbon confraternity. In his petition to Innocent XI, he claimed to be "procurator-general of the congregations of the Blacks and Mulattos of Our Lady of the

Rosary and of many other institutions".[18] We do not know if he had been or was still in touch with the confraternity in Bahia, but his concerns were remarkably repeated there a few years later when Paschoal Dias, a freed Black, was entrusted by the confraternity in Bahia to undertake a similar journey to Rome to submit a petition on behalf of Christian slaves, representing the "miserable state" in which they found themselves.[19]

The Confraternity of Our Lady Star of the Negroes, of which Lourenço da Silva was appointed procurator in Madrid in 1682, also enjoyed influential connections. It was recognized at the Spanish royal court, and the initiative in Lourenço's appointment was taken by Lorenzo de Re, a Knight of the Order of Christ, Master of the King's Music, a native of Lima then resident in the court of Madrid. Giacinto Rogio Monzon, an apostolic notary and chief notary of the royal chapel, declared that Lorenzo de Re, who was as well known to him as "an elder brother", claimed also to be a member of this confraternity,[20] but we know nothing else about it. Confraternities for Blacks had existed in Spain from the late sixteenth century, the oldest being founded in Cadiz in 1593; and another was started by twenty-four Blacks in Madrid in the middle of the eighteenth century,[21] but in Antonio Rumeu's work on Spanish brotherhoods there is no reference to that of Our Lady Star of the Negroes. Lourenço da Silva's appointment supplied him, however, with an additional, avowed reason for his visit to Rome. He was presenting himself before the pope, the cardinal datary or other curial officials, wrote Monzon, in order to obtain confirmation of the indulgences and other privileges bestowed upon the confraternity.

The affidavits which Lourenço brought with him to Rome from Lisbon and Madrid, therefore, clearly marked him as a respectable and leading representative of these Blacks of the African diaspora. But what was the real quest which took him to Rome? What was "the certain matter" concerning which he was hoping to petition the pope and which "many Mulattos from various parts" had come to discuss with the Lisbon notary, Gaspar da Costa, as he stated with reticence in his affidavit?[22] The only clue we have is a scrap of paper, approximately 12 centimetres by 6.5 centimetres, which is now bound together with these affidavits. Da Costa's affidavit had been folded tightly, apparently to enclose this "secret" document, the outer page of the affidavit (folio 493) being soiled along the folds, presumably as a result of Lourenço's travels in the two years it had taken him to reach Rome from Lisbon. On the little piece of paper, there is a note in Portuguese, written in quite a fair hand: "There is a book by João Bottero [sic] which at page 119 states that Paul IV in 1533 sent a brief so that the Indians in the West Indies should not be slaves".[23] The date is inaccurate; the pope involved is wrongly identified. In Book III of Part IV of the *Relationi universali* of Giovanni Botero there is a reference to a bull issued by Paul III in favour of the Indians, and Botero goes on to state that in 1543 the emperor ordered that Indians should not be made to work in the mines.[24] But the note treasured by Lourenço is of very great interest. It illuminates his world. It reveals that he came to Rome dominated by one passionate hope, and it proves conclusively that the petition which he presented to Innocent XI, although turned into sophisticated language by a Roman cleric,[25] sprang spontaneously from the overriding concerns of Lourenço and his fellow Blacks. He was in no way a front man for a bunch of humanitarian do-gooders.

It is possible that Lourenço had himself consulted Botero's work. More probably he had been given this information by someone else, perhaps even in the office of the notary in Lisbon. Somewhere in his wanderings and discussions, the fact had emerged that on one occasion, some 150 years earlier, a papal document had condemned a form of slavery. Armed with this apparently vital precedent, Lourenço, had come to Rome to demand justice. The scrap of paper establishes that he, and he alone, initiated in Rome what was to be by far the most significant debate ever held within the Curia concerning the iniquities of the Atlantic slave trade. Others in Rome, notably the Capuchins, were to take up and elaborate the charges, but the note and affidavits make it clear that Lourenço and his petition were not initially put forward by any pressure group in Rome itself. The crucial first initiative came from Lourenço, and from the Blacks with whom he had discussed the matter in Lisbon and else-where. His petition reveals, therefore, some of the deepest concerns of a harassed yet Christianized slave elite.

The principal thrust of Lourenço's petition was directed against the institution of perpetual slavery, especially when it involved Christians or, as the petition put it, those whom God had created and "with holy baptism had directed to-wards the enjoyment of eternal glory". He vividly described the cruelties inflicted on slaves, stating that they were pun-ished by being burnt "with sealing-wax, lard, resin, pitch and other materials". (The Portuguese verb *pingar* was, in-deed, commonly used to describe a punishment that consisted "of letting drops of hot molten fat or wax fall upon a slave's naked flesh".[26]) As a result of these and other cruelties, sim-ilar, Lourenço stated, to those used by the tyrants who per-secuted the primitive church, "innumerable souls of these Christian Blacks" were lost. When these people, "over-worked and subject to ill-treatment and punishments, see that not only they but also their children, even though they are white, are condemned to remain enslaved, they kill themselves in desperation". All this, Lourenço concluded, was the result of "the diabolic abuse of such slavery". His petition went on to remind the pope that his predecessors had issued various briefs on this matter, but they had been ignored. "In the name of all those oppressed", he requested that "those wretches who are involved in the sale and pur-chase of these unhappy Christians" should be placed under the severest excommunication, release from which would be reserved to the pope himself. Lourenço thought that by the publication of such a decree and by sending it to the inquisitors and bishops of the whole of Christendom, the pope would "liberate all these Christians, and increase in numbers all the more those who otherwise are being completely annihilated".[27]

Lourenço's petition was thus almost exclusively concerned with the fate of his fellow Christians, but his emphasis on the iniquity of perpetual slavery may have accurately re-flected the deepest anguish of all Africans entrapped in the Atlantic slave systems. He did not attempt to question the institution of slavery itself. Indeed many of those African peoples who by the late seventeenth century were exposed to the Atlantic slave trade accepted within their own societies various degrees of servitude. Yet seldom, if ever, was the status of slavery in African societies rigidly perpetuated over the generations. A slave's descendants in Africa could hope eventually to escape from the stigma and disadvantages of their origins. It was precisely the absence of such a hope which was the feature most bitterly criticized by Lourenço, in what must be one of the earliest recorded representations by the victims of the established pattern of Atlantic slavery. Significantly, the institution of perpetual slavery had also been one of the principal aspects of the Atlantic slave trade denounced by one of its first critics, Fernando Oliveira, in his *Arte do guerra do mar* published in 1555. Here Oliveira maintained that there was absolutely no moral justification for the children of African Christian slaves to be brought up as slaves. Lourenço made no reference to this work, but this is hardly surprising since Charles Boxer believes that Oliveria's book was "never quoted by contemporaries . . . and obviously it was ignored at Rome . . . its enlightened author was clearly a voice crying in the wilderness".[28]

The crucial significance of Lourenço's petition lay, however, not in his own somewhat limited concerns but in its immediate impact on curial officials. His intervention had the effect of raising far wider and more fundamental problems. His first-hand account of the cruelties inflicted on slaves caught the attention of the cardinals assembled at Propaganda Fide, the curial Congregation with responsibility for mission territories, to which Innocent XI had referred Lourenço petition. Other earlier reports from missionaries to the Congregation had denounced aspects of the slave trade,[29] but it seems as if Lourenço's presence in Rome and his impassioned plea presented at first hand had now suddenly opened the cardinals' eyes to the horrors which were being perpetrated on the outer fringes of their world. Archbishop Edoardo Cibo, the secretary of Propaganda Fide, in placing the matter before the meeting of its General Congregation of 6 March 1684, made it quite clear that he accepted the facts as stated by Lourenço. Prior to this meeting, he had interrogated two Spaniards and a Portuguese who had been missionaries "in those parts". They confirmed Lourenço's description and added further horrific details of the punishments meted out to recalcitrant slaves. They described how the slaves were savagely whipped, tortured by being greased and grilled "as meat is roasted by our cooks", and "other tyrannies so evil that many of these Negroes suffocate themselves . . . or hurl themselves into the sea to drown when they are free to do so". The missionaries also considered that the purchase of slaves involved Christian merchants in "iniquity and injustice". Often the slaves had been stolen from their mothers and taken by force to the ships, where they were brought by traders to "be sold as cattle". In other cases, the merchants bought them from Christians who went into the bush to hunt them "as game is hunted in Europe", killing those who resisted and keeping the others promiscuously so that "like animals they would be made to breed and produce greater profits".[30]

The focus had thus shifted from the fate of Christian slaves to cover a whole range of injustices committed by Christian traders and masters. The cardinals of the Congregation of Propaganda Fide decided to take immediate action. Later the same day, strongly worded letters were despatched to the nuncios in Madrid and Lisbon which clearly reflect the impact of Lourenço's petition:

New and urgent appeals on the part of the Negroes of the Indies to his holiness, and by him remitted to this holy Congregation, have caused no little bitterness to his holiness and their eminences on seeing that there still continues in those parts such a detestable abuse as to sell human blood, sometimes even with fraud and violence. This involves a disgraceful offence against Catholic liberty, by condemning to perpetual slavery not only those who are bought and sold, but also the sons and daughters who are born to them, although they have been made Christians.

To this is added an even greater grief on hearing how they are then so cruelly tormented that this results in the loss of innumerable souls, who are rendered desperate by such maltreatment perpetrated by those same Christians who should indeed protect and defend them; and, by the hatred which this conceives, the progress of missionaries in spreading the holy faith remains impeded.

The nunicos were therefore instructed earnestly to request the rulers of Spain and Portugal to order their officials overseas to prohibit under the severest penalties "such inhumanity as contrary to natural and civil law and much more to the gospel and sacred canons",[31] though, as will be seen, in responding to these instructions the nuncios were severely handicapped.

Perhaps partly because Lourenço claimed a royal Kongolese origin, the attention of Propaganda in this matter was particularly focused on that kingdom, and the discussion of his petition was listed under the leading "Congo". It was precisely in this area that the Capuchins were then undertaking what appeared to be one of their most promising missions, and of all Catholic missions in the seventeenth century those of the Capuchins were most readily open to the supervision and assistance of Propaganda Fide. On the same day that Archbishop Cibo wrote to the nuncios, he wrote also to the "prefect and missionaries of Congo", condemning the cruelty and evil inherent in the slave trade,[32] and in Rome the next move in the debate opened by Lourenço's initiative was in fact taken by the Capuchins.

A year after the meeting at which the cardinals had considered Lourenço's petition, they were again confronted with the issue of the Atlantic slave trade. At their meeting on 12 March 1685 they considered a long, undated memorandum which had been submitted to them by Capuchin missionaries. Like Lourenço's petition, this also is a fascinating document of fundamental importance. It is of startling originality, for it decisively broke away from the limits within which the ethics of the Atlantic slave trade had previously been discussed by the papacy. No longer was the argument concerned with the situation confronting Christians, but with rights arising from a common humanity.

The memorandum was signed by Giambattista Carampelli da Sabbio, who had been procurator-general of the Capuchins since 1678.[33] Some insight into his standing and influence in the papal Curia is provided in an unpublished account written by a Capuchin missionary, Giovanni Belotti da Romano, who in May 1680 had arrived in Rome charged with affairs concerning the Congo mission. With the help of Cardinal Alderano Cibo, secretary of state and the distinguished elder brother of Edoardo, secretary of Propaganda, Fra Giambattista had no difficulty in arranging "very quickly" an audience for Fra Giovanni with Innocent XI, who the same evening ordered Edoardo Cibo to give Fra Giovanni "every satisfaction".[34] The following year, Fra Giambattista had defended his order in a celebrated case in the Congregation of Bishops and Regulars, which had the effect of bringing him even closer to Innocent XI, "who admitted him into a close friendship".[35]

It was fortunate that the Capuchins' memorandum was backed by Fra Giambattista's authority and influence, for among its other principal authors were, most probably, two Capuchin missionaries whose standing had recently been placed in doubt. One was a Spaniard, Francisco de Jaca, the other a Frenchman, Epiphane de Moirans. Both had been excommunicated in Havana in 1681 and subsequently arrested for behaviour which had resulted, so reported the local authorities, "in the gravest scandals". They had preached that "the owners of Negro slaves should liberate them and their children and pay them for their labours", and they had refused to give absolution to those who did not promise to do this.[36] Both Capuchins had written defences of their position. Fray Francisco's statement is a vibrant denunciation of the abuses and injustices that he had witnessed; Père Epiphane was a competent canon lawyer and his statement marshals at length the case against the Atlantic slave trade. He quotes from a formidable range of authorities, but he also draws vividly on his own experiences. He had lost no opportunities to collect relevant data, and while he had been in Lisbon, he had discussed the situation in Africa with Capuchins serving in the Congo mission.[37] Transported from Havana to Cadiz, they eventually managed to come to Rome. With the support of Fra Giambattista, Fray Francisco de Jaca presented a petition to Propaganda on behalf of the American Indians, and undoubtedly they had helped to draft the Capuchins' memorandum on Black slavery, which was considered immediately after Fray Francisco's petition at the General Congregation of 12 March 1685.

The strategy of the Capuchins' memorandum was crystal clear. They made no attempt to question the institution of slavery itself, accepted by Aristotle and enshrined in Roman law. Instead they insisted implicitly on the distinction between "just" enslavement, which resulted from the punishment of certain crimes or capture in a "just" war, and other forms of unjust servitude. In the conditions prevailing in Africa and the Americas, this was a vital, if theoretical, distinction. The thrust of their memorandum was directed against the fraudulent and unjust ways in which slaves were obtained in Africa, against traders who made no attempt to ascertain whether slaves had been justly enslaved or not, against the dangers and horrors of the middle passage and against the owners of salves who held them, together with their children, under inhuman conditions in the Americas. Faced with these evils, the Capuchins requested the cardinals to condemn these abuses specifically listed in eleven propositions. The first three condemned both the enslavement by violence and fraud of innocent "Negroes and other natives", and also their purchase and sale even when they were sold together with those who had justly been deprived of their liberty. The next three made it necessary for anyone purchasing slaves to ascertain beforehand whether the reasons for their servitude were just, for owners to emancipate innocent slaves, and for both owners and traders to pay them compensation. In addition to these drastic limitations to the slave trade as it was practised, the seventh proposition forbade the owners of slaves to endanger, wound or kill them on their private authority.

If implemented, the effect of these propositions would have been even more drastic than the reforms earlier advocated by the Jesuit, Alonso de Sandoval. And it was equally significant that the Capuchins' plea was grounded solely in humanitarian concern or, as they themselves put it, they were motivated only "by Christian charity".[38] Whereas earlier papal documents[39] had merely condemned the sale of Christians, the Capuchins made no distinction between persons on the ground of religion. None of these seven propositions made the slightest distinction between Christian and other slaves, and only the remaining four were concerned with the questions of instructing slaves before and after baptism, of keeping them in concubinage, of manumission and of the sale of slaves to heretics. Taken as a whole, the memorandum was a skilful and radical plea for justice against a massive violation of basic human rights.

The Congregation of Propaganda Fide, although powerful and autonomous in other respects, did not, have the authority to decide theological or ethical issues. The eleven propositions submitted by the Capuchins were therefore forwarded the same day to the assessor of the Holy Office with the request that they should be examined and that suitable resolutions should be taken.[40] For over a year, nothing more was heard of the matter. Such a delay was by no means unusual. Indeed Francesco Ingoli, the first secretary of Propaganda Fide, had in vain attempted to wrest this power from the Holy Office, precisely because he had experienced similar problems and delays.[41]

It was at this stage that Lourenço da Silva made a further, decisive intervention. At the General Congregation of Propaganda Fide held on 14 January 1686, a petition was submitted to the cardinals on behalf of "the Blacks and Mulattos born of Christian parents both in Brazil and in the city of Lisbon". The petition was not presented by Lourenço in person, nor did it mention his name. He is, however, referred to by name as being responsible for it in the letters subsequently sent to the nuncios and bishops.[42] This time the petition was focused solely on the fate of these Christians in Brazil and Lisbon, all of them baptized, but held by "White Christians who make contracts to sell them in different places . . . like so many animals". Desperately the petitioners appealed to a common identity based, not on pigment which was insidiously to obliterate other values, but on religion, on "the seal of holy baptism, not being of Jewish race nor pagans, but only following the Catholic faith, like any and every Christian, as is known to all". The petition referred to the argument that Whites were entitled by a papal brief, granted "for a limited and long past time", to conduct "similar Negro peoples into the Catholic faith and to retain them for that time as slaves".[43] But, the petition robustly argued, it was not thereby conceded that these Negroes "nor their children, nor their children's children should remain slaves in perpetuity". Shrewdly the petition mobilized religious and racial prejudice by mentioning that some of these Christian slaves were even purchased and held by "occult Jews". The petition appealed therefore to the papacy to declare that:

> no one who has received the water of holy baptism should remain a slave, and all those who have been born or would be born to Christian parents should remain free, under pain of excommunication ... remembering that God sent His own Son to redeem humanity and that He was crucified.[44]

Ignoring the particular concern of this petition with the fate of baptized slaves. Archbishop Cibo nevertheless seized the opportunity to remind the cardinals that in order to prevent "similar illicit contracts" the Capuchins had submitted eleven propositions which had been sent to the Holy Office, but "no one knew what decisions had been taken about them".[45] The cardinals decided to write again to the Holy Office. The Capuchins had drafted their propositions with care, and on 20 March 1686 the Holy Office formally declared its complete agreement with every proposition.[46] No longer was it the case of a lone Jesuit or maverick Capuchins measuring themselves against the slave trade. The highest tribunal of the Roman Curia had now promulgated a set of formidable and rigorous condemnations, covering a whole range of abuses. The debate initiated by Lourenço had been brought to a triumphant conclusion. His own somewhat limited concerns had been swept up into a far wider challenge. The doubts and hesitations expressed by the defenders of the status quo had been set aside. The Atlantic slave trade as it was actually operating had been officially condemned in the clearest possible way.

The sequel, however, was almost total anticlimax. Archbishop Cibo quickly sent the resolutions of the Holy Office to the bishops of Angola, Cadiz, Valencia, Seville and Malaga, and also to the nuncios in Spain and Portugal, with orders that these decisions should be enforced by the priests and missionaries in their dioceses.[47] The archbishop did not, however, order the nuncios to request the intervention of the Spanish and Portuguese crowns, as he had done under the initial impact of Lourenço's first petition. Nor was the papal power of excommunication specifically invoked as Lourenço had requested. Perhaps something of the urgency felt so acutely in 1684 under the immediate shock of the horrific disclosures had been lost. The Atlantic slave trade, for all its evils and abuses, was a remote phenomenon only occasionally impinging directly on the consciousness of the authorities in Rome. Even in Propaganda Fide it was but one issue among the many other problems which demanded the immediate attention of the cardinals and their officials.

Moreover the crowns of Spain and Portugal vigorously resisted any diminution of their patronal rights over ecclesiastical affairs. In 1684 when responding to Propaganda's first letter on the subject, the nuncios in both Madrid and Lisbon had underlined the difficulties of any reform and the need to rely on royal officials.[48] Indeed exactly at the same time as Rome was considering the protests of Lourenço and the propositions of the Capuchins, the Council of the Indies in Spain was curtly rebutting the attempted intervention of the nuncio in a complicated case involving a contract with a Dutch slave trader.[49] The Holy Office could define questions of ethics, but the enforcement of its decisions depended on clerics and laity whose immediate ecclesiastical, and ultimate political, loyalties lay elsewhere.

The *patronato* was but one indication of the way in which the church had been moulded by the social and economic structures of Europe and of European expansion overseas. In the seventeenth, as in other centuries, the church was not only the church of the poor and the oppressed, of those whom Lourenço and the Capuchins represented. It was also the church of the privileged and of the conquistadores. This aspect of reality was voiced right at the beginning of this particular debate on the slave trade. Among the documents considered by Propaganda Fide before the General Congregation of 6 March 1684 was an anonymous memorandum headed "Instructions for Mgr Cybo". Reflecting the reactions of an experienced and worldly-wise ecclesiastic, it may well have been the work of Archbishop Cibo's elder and distinguished brother. The second-born son of an aristocratic family whose power had recently increased, Cardinal Alderano Cibo had entered the conclave of 1676 as a *papabile*.[50] A close friend of the man who was in fact elected, he was immediately made secretary of state, a post he held throughout the pontificate of Innocent XI. As we have seen, when Fra Giovanni da Romano visited Rome, Cardinal Cibo showed a keen interest in the work of the Capuchin missionaries. It is therefore very probable that he had seen Lourenço's first petition before it was forwarded to Propaganda, and the tone of the memorandum is one of advice from a superior ecclesiastic, accustomed to corresponding with the nuncios.

These anonymous "Instructions" began by throwing considerable doubts on the facts as presented by Lourenço. Pointing out that a slave cost 600 or more Spanish dollars, the author maintained that this would normally be sufficient to induce owners to care for slaves "as if they were sons". If, however, "a slave acted in a bestial way against his master, it was necessary to punish him severely in the most forceful manner by scalding him, as with cattle, otherwise he would kill his master as had happened on many occasions". Such treatment, this representative of the voice of the rich maintained, would, however, be an exception rather than the rule. The author agreed that the nuncio in Lisbon could be asked to make representations so that those who stole Blacks in Africa unjustly would be severely punished and excommunicated. Responding to Lourenço's specific request, he also envisaged ways in which the children of baptized slaves could be set at liberty, if the price paid for their fathers was reduced in anticipation of this reform. But he underlined "America's great need for Negroes, whether for cultivating the land or for work in the mines, for no other people could survive that heat and labour", and he warned that any reform would be difficult as the king of Spain received "very large sums from the tolls levied on such sales".[51]

This anonymous memorandum was a cool and realistic evaluation of the forces ranged against Lourenço, the Capuchins and the Holy Office. Yet, under the impact of Lourenço's protest, the cardinals and secretary of Propaganda Fide had gone far beyond these instructions and had sought to launch a radical attack on the abuses of the slave trade. The document, however, helps to explain why they failed and why the vested interests involved continued to ignore their strictures. Only when Christians came to question the status of slavery itself, as some Quakers were beginning to do during the last quarter of the seventeenth century, would the attack on the slave trade gradually become widespread. The resolutions of the Holy Office were in practice largely ignored; but they were not forgotten. On several occasions during the eighteenth century and as late as 1821, Propaganda Fide referred enquirers, and itself appealed, to the principles enunicated in 1686;[52] but this was no consolation for the descendants of those for whom Lourenço and the Capuchins had campaigned.

CHAPTER 2

Fra Girolamo, Propaganda Fide and the Atlantic Slave Trade

The reports concerning the coastal kingdoms of West Central Africa published by Capuchin missionaries were much the most important contributions by any group of Italians to Europe's knowledge of sub-Saharan Africa in the seventeenth and eighteenth centuries. Their achievement has been thoroughly described and justly praised,[1] and historians, ethnographers and other scholars concerned with African studies are increasingly returning to this rich mine of information. The *Breve e succinta relatione del viaggio nel regno del Congo nell'Africa meridionale* by Fra Girolamo Merolla da Sorrento, published in Naples in 1692, is in at least one respect one of the most interesting of these accounts. Although Fra Girolamo inevitably shared many of the ethnocentric and cultural prejudices of his colleagues, his description of life in Soyo, the region of Kongo situated at the mouth of the River Zaire, displays a warm and enthusiastic appreciation of the Christians of the area. His sympathy and deep friendship with many of his congregation illuminates his book, and the detailed information which he provides enables one to begin to reassess the process of religious and social change which was then taking place in that region. His account clearly portrays the depth and extent to which Christianity was penetrating into the life and culture of Soyo's ruling elite (see below, Chapter 3).

It is, however, also a fact, the implications of which have for long been misunderstood, that in the complex history of the papacy's response to the development of the Atlantic slave trade, a small yet tragically significant role was played by this Neapolitan priest. Set against the mammoth scale of human misery involved in this traffic which so greatly

shaped the development of the world's economy, Fra Girolamo's role seems almost trivial. Yet it vividly illustrates the
difficulties of accurate communication between Europe and
Africa in this early period. Europe's ignorance of African
realities was but seldom pierced. Yet when for an instant the
leaders of the church caught a glimpse of the horrors of the
slave trade and were briefly determined to attempt to eradicate them, their intentions were obscured in Africa itself by
the concerns and convictions of their local emisssaries, Fra
Girolamo and his superior. Europe's knowledge of Africa
was minimal; its capacity to rectify its relations with "the
Dark Continent" was correspondingly restricted.

In his book, Fra Girolamo recounts how in the second
year of his mission (1684), when he was alone in Soyo,
"l'Illustrissimo, e Reverendissimo Monsignor Cibo" wrote,
"on behalf of the Sacred Congregation", deploring the fact
that in the Kingdom of Kongo there still continued "the
abominable and most pernicious abuse of selling slaves,
principally Christians, to heretics".[2] Fra Girolamo's statement achieved widespread, if inaccurate, publicity. In the
English translation, published in 1704 and often reprinted,
the author of the letter from Rome was reported as "the
most Reverend Cardinal Cibo" who had written "in the
name of the Sacred College".[3] This attribution was followed
in the French translation by Prévost, where the date was
given erroneously as 1683,[4] and in turn by the canon lawyer,
Domingo Muriel S.J.,[5] which Margraf[2] followed by Pastor[7]
elaborated into an initiative taken by Innocent XI. It is quite
clear, however, that Fra Girolamo must have been referring
to a letter written by Archbishop Edoardo Cibo. A younger
brother of the famous Cardinal Alderano Cibo, (see above p.
26), Edoardo Cibo was secretary of the Congregation of
Propaganda Fide from 1680 to 1695. A cardinal would not
have been referred to as "Illustrissimo e Reverendissimo
Monsignor", nor would Cardinal Cibo have written "da
parte della Sacra Congregazione", as Fra Girolamo originally stated.

In the archives of Propaganda Fide, there is indeed a copy
of a letter sent by Archbishop Edoardo Cibo to the "Prefect
and missionaries of Congo" on 6 March 1684.[8] The letter

does not, however, contain any mention of the "pernicious abuse of selling slaves ... to heretics", as Fra Girolamo maintained in his book, which remained of course the only published account of Rome's initial action on this matter. The practice of selling slaves to heretics had indeed been condemned in previous pronouncements from Propaganda Fide, but the letter of 1684 in fact represented a dramatic and fundamental break in the approach of the papacy to the moral problems raised by the Atlantic slave trade. Neither Muriel, Margraf nor Pastor, basing themselves on the text and mistranslation of Fra Girolamo, present anything like a correct appreciation of the profound change of course advocated by the papacy.

Moved by Lourenço da Silva's first petition (see above, p. 12), Archbishop Cibo informed the missionaries that it had caused the Sacred Congregation "infinite displeasure to hear that not only did the pernicious abuse of selling and buying Negroes continue in those regions, but also that there was exercised against them such inhumane cruelty that innumerable souls are lost". The missionaries were ordered therefore not to fail "to represent to these Peoples the gravity of such sin", and they were instructed to use "every means and attention to eradicate such as abuse ... assuring those Christians that, although abstaining from such sale and purchase would deprive them of that little gain which they derive from it, much greater would be the reward of their souls by conforming to this admonition".[9]

Although the language is somewhat opaque, it is clear that the archbishop's letter condemned not the sale of slaves to heretics but the cruelty and evil inherent in the trade itself. Why then was Fra Girolamo so convinced that the letter condemned the "pernicious abuse" of selling Christian slaves to heretics? It is just possible that Fra Girolamo drew this conclusion himself, but it is far more probable that this interpretation of Propaganda's instructions was given him by the missionary who had just taken over the prefecture in Luanda. Fra Girolamo states that he came to know of Archbishop Cibo's letter only after Fra Giuseppe Maria da Busseto had left Soyo to take over direction of the mission in Luanda after the death of the prefect, Fra Giovanni Belotti da

Romano, who seems to have died on 29 November 1684.[10] Presumably Fra Giuseppe Maria either found Cibo's letter on his arrival at Luanda or it must have reached him soon after he took up his duties there. And it seems very likely indeed that his own previous experiences and his assessment of the political situation facing the mission would have led him to give Fra Girolamo this narrow and mistaken inter-pretation of Propaganda's new intentions.

Fra Giuseppe Maria had had many years of work both in the Portuguese settlements of Luanda and Massangano and also in the mission at Soyo. He had reached Luanda in August 1668 and had undertaken the first of several visits to Soyo in April 1669.[11] In particular he had played a crucial role in re-establishing the Capuchins in Soyo after they had been temporarily expelled following some traumatic events in 1670. In that year, the Portuguese in Luanda had sent a powerful army to invade and conquer Soyo. In the first engagement, the ruler of Soyo was mortally wounded and his army routed. Soon afterwards, however, the Soyo army rallied and overwhelmed the Portuguese invaders, killing the commanding officers and taking many captives together with much valuable booty.[12] The events had however left the people of Soyo deeply antagonistic to the Portuguese, and for various reasons tensions between the ruler of Soyo and the Capuchin missionaries had increased, coming to a head on Christmas Day 1673 when two priests had been forcibly expelled.

At this critical moment, Fra Giuseppe Maria had been sent from Luanda to ascertain if a reconciliation was possible. After five days of negotiation at Mpinda, the port of Soyo, he had been received triumphantly into the province's capital and had persuaded the ruler to sign a series of capitulations which protected the future of the mission.[13] Ten years later, when he returned yet again to Soyo taking Fra Girolamo with him, he was again welcomed with signs of great en-thusiasm, and this time he was able to persuade Antonio II Barreto da Silva, ruler of Soyo 1680–91, to consider opening negotiations for re-establishing peace with the Portuguese. This was a diplomatic triumph which he considered to be of vital importance for the progress of the whole mission, as he explained to the cardinals of Propaganda Fide in a letter written soon after he had returned to Luanda to take up the duties of vice-prefect. This letter provides us with a clear indication of his strategic thinking at the time when he received Archbishop Cibo's letter concerning the slave trade. The mission was being seriously weakened by the civil wars which were destroying the kingdom of Kongo. Soyo had been the gate through which the Faith had first entered the kingdom and, Fra Giuseppe Maria hoped, "it would again be the gate for its restoration". The ruler of Soyo was "very powerful" and was "greatly feared" throughout the kingdom. He would be feared even more when "*Li Grandi di Congo*" would see him united in peace and friendship with the Portuguese, and Fra Giuseppe Maria was confident that the nobility of Kongo would then resolve to elect a Catholic king. Besides this great prize, peace between Soyo and the Portuguese could result in yet another advantage. Such a peace could eliminate the sale by Soyo of so many baptized souls to "heretics, particularly the English, who carry them off to Barbados, their colony, and thus again it could meet the wishes of this Sacred Tribunal".[14]

It is clear, therefore, that for Fra Giuseppe Maria, Archbishop Cibo's call to eradicate the cruelties and abuses of the slave trade could best be met immediately by seeking to eliminate the sale of slaves to heretics. He was also convinced that, by themselves, the Capuchins in Luanda and Kongo could achieve little against the slave trade as a whole. This conviction was set out in a letter written two years later, which may well have been a reply to yet further admonitions from Rome concerning the slave trade.

We do not know when Propaganda's letter instructing the Bishop of Angola with the priests and missionaries in his diocese to enforce the decisions of the Holy Office of 20 March 1686 (see above, p. 24) actually reached Luanda. It seems possible, however, that Fra Giuseppe Maria had heard of them before writing to Propaganda Fide on 8 March 1687. Complaining that almost three years had passed since the death of the prefect and that still no new missionaries had been sent to the mission, Fra Giuseppe Maria went on to point out to the cardinals that it was for him an impossible task to eliminate the abuse of selling and buying slaves, because here the Religious are engaged in it, particularly the Jesuits, who have a boat which every year goes to Brazil laden with slaves; hence only Your Eminences together with His Holiness can remove such an abuse by writing to the King of Portugal concerning this affair.[15]

It would be mistaken to conclude that Fra Giuseppe Maria sought merely to wash his hands of all the problems connected with the slave trade. Manifestly he believed that the mission depended on the Portuguese for its effectiveness. It was not simply that the rights of the *Padroado* gave the Portuguese crown control over ecclesiastical affairs within its "conquests". It was also the fact that by the late seventeenth century the Capuchins travelled to their mission on Portuguese ships, and that Luanda, the see of the Bishop of Congo and Angola, was a sizeable community of at least nominal Christians and the sole source of various essential goods, such as the few European medicines which were available on the Central African coast, a point that Fra Giuseppe Maria had made in an earlier memorandum to Propaganda.[16] Yet his alliance with the local Portuguese, and his willingness to further their interests, was also combined with a firm commitment to the mission in Soyo and a warm appreciation of the Christian community there. Like Fra Girolamo, he was moved by the faith of the Christians in Soyo.[17] In attempting to assist the Portuguese, he was not seeking to destroy this flourishing community, and one of his colleagues helped Antonio II to resist successfully Portuguese demands for the construction of a fort at the port of Mpinda.[18] Nor is there reason to think that Fra Giuseppe Maria was unconcerned with the abuses and evils perpetrated in the sale and purchase of innocent slaves. Placed as he was, he felt himself powerless even to begin to confront these basic evils of the trade which was bringing Europe and Africa together in so disastrous a union.

We can, therefore, be reasonably certain that when Fra Girolamo launched his attack in Soyo on the sale of slaves to heretics, he was responding to his superior's interpretation of the wishes of Archbishop Cibo. It was none the less a sadly ironic consequence of Propaganda's initiative. In his book, Fra Girolamo describes how his demands led to conflict between himself and Antonio II,[19] and these incidents were but the first stage of a continuing argument and source of tension between the missionaries and the rulers of Soyo.[20] Fra Girolamo himself, after returning to Italy, was to set sail again from Naples in 1692, the year his book was published, to take back reinforcements for the mission. These reinforcements were financed by a generous gift of 200 ducats from a Neapolitan canon with the promise of similar help in subsequent years,[21] though Fra Girolamo died in Luanda in 1697. But the hard and tragic fact remains that the only immediate consequence in Africa of the papacy's freshly aroused concern over the Atlantic slave trade, as expressed in Cibo's letter, was to introduce into Soyo, the most promising Catholic mission in Africa at that time, an element of conflict and tension which continued to embitter and weaken the relations between the missionaries and the local Christian rulers. During the eighteenth century the Atlantic slave trade inexorably expanded, dominating Europe's relations with Africa. The decisions promulgated by the Holy Office on 20 March 1686 continued to be ignored. The failure of this early initiative, and the misinterpretation of Propaganda's intentions, form therefore a sombre prologue to this tragedy. Europe's knowledge of African realities, and its ability to alter its contacts with the continent, remained tenuous in the extreme.

CHAPTER 3

Come vero Prencipe Catolico: the Capuchins and the Rulers of Soyo in the Late Seventeenth Century[1]

Students of Europe's contact with Africa have long regarded the Christian missions in the ancient kingdom of Kongo as a peculiarly potent symbol. For some the conversion and subsequent reign of Afonso I in the first half of the sixteenth century were a momentary aberration, a false dawn quickly to be obscured by the realities of the exploitation associated with mercantile capitalism and the horrors of the Atlantic slave trade. For others, the story of these missions has merely served to illustrate the continuing inviolability of indigenous traditions. Kongo society, it is argued, accepted only a thin veneer of Christianity, while its basic cosmology, practices and beliefs remained unchanged.

> Christianity affected only a slim minority. For the majority of the people of the Kongo, its ceremonies, its symbolism, its churches, and its clergy were less pretexts for belief than occasions for imitation. It left a lasting impression only where it managed to become associated with traditional usages. In trying to reach the people, it became an instrument of syncretism .... Alongside a Christianity which was weakly established and in constant danger, the traditional religious pluralism and the syncretic cults oriented the religious life of the people of the Kongo from the sixteenth century on.[2]

These interpretations share a common assumption. Faced with what seems to be the virtual extinction of Christianty in the area by the mid-nineteenth century, scholars have assumed that the early missionary impact was fleeting and superficial, and that these missions met with insuperable

difficulties or proceeded on false principles which inevitably involved them in failure. Yet the early influence of
Christianity in Kongo cannot be usefully discussed without
taking into account the fact that its impact varied enormously over time and space. At the capital, Mbanza Kongo
or San Salvador, the role of Christian missionaries was very
different in the reigns of Afonso I, or Garcia II (1641–61), or
Pedro IV (1696–1718), while in the various regions of the
kingdom there were even greater differences. If we take our
standpoint in the late seventeenth century and consider carefully the evidence for that period, we are confronted in
Soyo, a powerful, dominant region at that moment, not
with failure but with an extraordinary depth and extent of
Christian influence. Several factors distinguished Soyo from
the rest of Kongo, yet so striking is the picture of Soyo's
commitment to Christianity at this period that one is forced
to reconsider the whole direction of religious change that
was occurring at that moment. And, in doing so, one has to
begin to reassess some of the previous interpretations of this
major episode of Christian evangelism in Africa.

THE EMERGENCE OF SOYO

Soyo (Sogno, Sohio) was distinguished from the rest of the
kingdom of Kongo by its natural resources, its geographical
location and its historical development in the sixteenth and
seventeenth centuries. According to a Capuchin from Pavia,
Soyo was as large as the seventeenth-century state of Milan.[3]
It stretched along the Atlantic coast northwards from the
River Mbridge to the mouth of the Zaïre and inland along
the southern bank of this vast estuary. It was a sandy, relatively infertile area, whose principal natural product was
salt obtained on the sea-coast,[4] but from the end of the fifteenth century it was no longer a backwater. Its economic
and strategic importance was suddenly transformed. The
port of Mpinda, a few miles within the Zaïre estuary, provided the natural gateway for trade and contacts with the
Portuguese, and the capital of Soyo, Mbanza Soyo, was

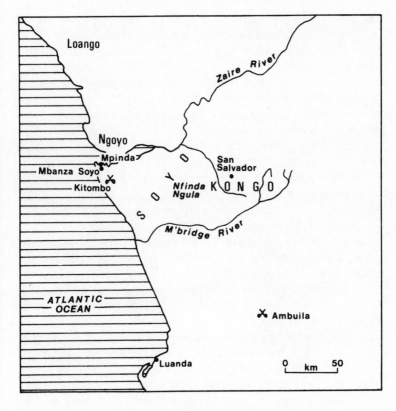

Soyo in the late seventeenth century.

established some three miles in the interior behind Mpinda. By the seventeenth century the ruler of Soyo was asserting a degree of independence which at times culminated in active revolt against the king of Kongo. This insubordination was assisted by the existence of the Nfinda Ngula, a large, forested wilderness which separated Soyo from Kongo,[5] but of even greater importance was the growth of trade with the Dutch.

After the Portuguese settlement in Luanda in the 1570s, the main commercial route of the *pombeiros* (trading agents of the Portuguese) between the Pool, San Salvador and

Luanda ran overland bypassing Soyo, but with the arrival of Dutch traders in the coastal kingdoms north of the Zaïre and in the Zaïre estuary in the 1590s, the fortunes of Soyo rapidly expanded. Unlike the Portuguese, the Dutch were willing to exchange firearms and ammunition for ivory, copper and slaves.[6] In the 1630s the army of Soyo defeated that of the king of Kongo on several occasions and Soyo became a haven for defeated, dissident factions from San Salvador,[7] but it was only in the last third of the seventeenth century that Soyo emerged as a dominant power in the Kongo kingdom.

In 1665 the Portuguese advancing from Luanda defeated the Kongo army, killing the king and many of his nobility at the battle of Ambuila. Only a few months later the ruler of Soyo seized his opportunity to ransack San Salvador and place his protégé on the Kongo throne, an intervention which was repeated in 1669. The following year the Portuguese governor in Luanda sent an army to invade and humble the upstart Soyo. After an initial defeat, however, the forces of Soyo rallied and, with Dutch armaments, smashed the Portuguese at Kitombo in October 1670, killing the Portuguese commander and taking many captives and much booty. It was a decisive victory. Not until the nineteenth century were the Portuguese again able to invade Kongo.[8] Yet Mbanza Soyo was never able to take the place of San Salvador: it never provided the central focus for the whole kingdom of Kongo, nor did its rulers ever attain the luxury, power and life-style previously enjoyed by the powerful Kongo kings. There is nothing in the late seventeenth-century descriptions of Soyo to match the magnificence of Garcia II's reception of the Dutch envoys in 1642.[9] But by the 1680s Soyo was definitely thought to be the key to peace and prosperity throughout Kongo: its rulers were reported to be "very powerful" and "greatly feared" by the prominent people in Kongo.[10]

The missionary records of the late seventeenth century give the impression that in Soyo local power was concentrated on the ruler and his court at Mbanza Soyo. The principal office holders were the ruler's close kinsmen, and if news of his illness became public a succession crisis could be

feared. The ruler could appoint and dismiss the governors
(*mani*) of dependent towns and villages at will, and after one
serious armed dispute with the captain-general of his army,
in which the Capuchins acted as mediators, he took care to
demote his opponents.[11] In so far as these sources provide an
insight into the political structure and organization of Soyo
in this period, they corroborate MacGaffey's opinion that
"the precolonial Kongo chief was much like the 'Big Man'
of Melanesia . . . a successful competitor in an unstable
political system" in which, however, favourable conditions
(as in late seventeenth-century Soyo) could for a period
produce "centralized, hierarchical and relatively stable regimes", while in the exercise of such power the existence
of a centre was "much more important" than clear territorial
boundaries.[12]

THE CAPUCHINS' ADVANTAGES IN SOYO

The Capuchins in Soyo were therefore probably correct in
concentrating their efforts at Mbanza Soyo, and as the power
of the rulers of Soyo increased so was the commitment of
Soyo to Christianity extended and intensified. When the first
Capuchin missionaries arrived at Mpinda in 1645 Soyo was
already in their eyes a Catholic country. They were welcomed amidst scenes of great enthusiasm by the populace
and ruler. A Dutch sea-captain attempted to prevent their
landing, but Soyo, together with rest of Kongo as exemplified by Garcia II,[13] showed little or no sympathy for Cal-
vinist doctrines, however much the ruler and people of Soyo
profited from Dutch commercial contacts. Hundreds of
people brought their children and youths to be baptized, and
the Capuchins throughout the seventeenth century did not
hesitate to distinguish sharply Soyo and Kongo from their
northern "pagan" neighbours.

As the missionaries subsequently attempted to enforce the
precepts of canon law, they soon encountered widespread
opposition in Soyo, as in the rest of the Kongo kingdom. In
Soyo, however, the Capuchins enjoyed peculiar advantages.
In the first place, they were able to establish and maintain
a continuous presence at Mbanza Soyo. Death and disease

took a steady toll of the missionaries who arrived after 1645, and the arrival of reinforcements was sporadic after the first few years, so that elsewhere in Kongo, outside San Salvador, it was rare for any provincial centre to have a resident missionary for more than a few years at a time, particularly after the 1650s. But in Mbanza Soyo there were always one or two Capuchin priests, ably assisted by a brother, one of whom, Leonardo da Nardo, through prolonged service obtained a deep knowledge of the people and their language.[14]

Even more important than this uninterrupted ministry, however, was the fact that in Soyo the Capuchins had no rivals. When the Capuchin missionaries arrived at San Salvador, there were several secular priests, of both Kongo and of mixed race. With many of these local priests the Capuchins were involved in bitter disputes over ecclesiastical jurisdiction. Inevitably this rivalry weakened their influence both with the king and other laity.[15] In Soyo, however, the Capuchins were the sole, unchallenged providers of Catholic sacraments, save for a few months in 1673–4 when Flemish Franciscans and a Kongolese priest briefly intruded into their monopoly.[16]

THE DIPLOMATIC ROLE OF THE CAPUCHINS

Throughout the seventeenth century the Capuchins in Soyo, as in Kongo, derived some of their influence from the particular position they occupied in the wider diplomatic world. They had been sent to Kongo by Pope Urban VIII in response to repeated overtures from the kings of Kongo who had long been attempting to establish a direct contact with Rome. The kings wanted to receive missionaries who would be independent of the Portuguese *padroado*, and it was no coincidence that the Sacred Congregation of Propaganda Fide selected the Capuchins for this task as theirs was the Order most closely identified with this new, powerful curial organ, by which the papacy hoped to assert its influence over Catholic missionary activity. The first parties of Spanish, Flemish and Italian Capuchins had slipped into Mpinda while the Dutch had temporarily occupied Luanda. After the reconquest of Luanda in 1648 the Portuguese crown was prepared to continue to admit Italian Capuchins to this mission field provided that they were not Spanish subjects and that they passed through Lisbon and Luanda. In Kongo the Capuchins became something of a diplomatic liability for Garcia II after 1648,[17] but the rulers of Soyo continued to appreciate the diplomatic benefits which could be drawn from these contacts with the missionaries from Rome.

Although the Portuguese in Luanda were defeated in their attempt to conquer Soyo in 1670, they still remained an ominous, hostile force, and the ruler of Soyo requested the pope to intervene on his behalf. As a result the papal nuncio elicited from the king of Portugal an admission that the ruler of Soyo was an independent prince. The nuncio also received an assurance from the king that the hostility of the governor of Luanda towards Soyo did not reflect the policy of Lisbon.[18] Firearms and artillery obtained from Dutch traders were undoubtedly the principal external factor in ensuring the survival of an independent Soyo, and, as will be seen, the rulers of Soyo thoroughly appreciated the crucial importance of maintaining access to these weapons. It is also clear, however, that the rulers were anxious not to become entirely dependent on the Dutch. The links with papal diplomacy provided Soyo with an independent access, however tenuous and slight, to the world of European diplomacy, and this brought distinct, if intangible, advantages.

The Capuchins also played a major role in the protracted negotiations which eventually led to a re-establishment of relations between Soyo and the Portuguese. As early as 1685 the vice-prefect of the mission could report that the ruler of Soyo, "*Come vero Prencipe Catolico*", was prepared for the church to take a major part in this critical diplomacy.[19] While patiently assisting the Portuguese to strengthen their contacts with Soyo, the Capuchins steadfastly supported the ruler in his refusal to permit the Portuguese to establish a fort at the strategic port of Mpinda. They seem to have accomplished this task with at least a touch of that skill and charity which enabled members of their order to play similar roles in the diplomacy of seventeenth-century Europe,[20] and for more than a decade the Capuchins were intimately involved in the execution of Soyo's foreign policy.[21]

THE CAPUCHINS AND THE SOYO AUTHORITIES

The influence of the Capuchins in Soyo, however, was not solely, or even principally, due to their undoubted political and diplomatic value to the state. Far more fundamentally they possessed a basic, ritual significance. They were welcomed and respected as Christian priests who made accessible what were increasingly recognized as sacraments of salvation by Soyo's rulers and their subjects. As in any example of profound and extensive interaction between an African polity and Christian missionary activity, points of congruence were found between the new religion and the local social structures. In the Kongo kingdom as a whole the Capuchins occupied an ambivalent position. In most of the kingdom the points of congruence fluctuated and were unstable. At times, particularly for the first three years of their mission, the Capuchins saw themselves, and were seen by the ruler and people of Kongo, as allied to the king and his local representatives; at other times, especially when they later came into open conflict with Garcia II, they were seen as the opponents of hostile and "oppressive" rulers.[22] In Soyo, although elements of tension between rulers and missionaries remained, as one might expect if evangelism preserved its potential prophetic challenge, the Capuchins were far more closely and continuously identified with the establishment, and in its turn, the ruling institution at the centre of Soyo became far more thoroughly Christianized than was the case with the government centred on San Salvador in the seventeenth century.

Most of the principal public rituals in Soyo were becoming centred around the Christian calendar by the late seventeenth century. The festivals of Easter, Christmas, Pentecost and All Souls had become major occasions, uniting ruler and subjects in colourful, enthusiastic displays of worship and rejoicing. On such occasions the ruler attended Mass splendidly arrayed in the white robes of the Order of Christ. Even on weekdays (for he normally attended church at least three times a week, either for Mass or the Rosary) he came specially attired, wearing on his breast a cross of solid gold, holding his rods of office and borne aloft in a hammock. He was accompanied by a crowd of attendants, who carried his velvet-covered chair, his faldstool, carpet and cushion, and he was preceded by musicians sounding trumpets, double-bells and other instruments. During Mass, before the reading of the Gospel, one of his pages was given a lighted torch, and at the end of the Gospel the missal was brought to him to kiss. At the end of Mass he came forward to the altar to receive benediction and accompanied the priest into the sacristy.[23]

Besides these regular occasions for regal splendour and royal ritual participation, two saints' days had become of great local political significance. As in Kongo, every governor (*mani*) or headman of the towns and major villages of Soyo was obliged to present himself at Mbanza Soyo accompanied "by all his people" to hear Mass and to render obedience to the ruler on the feast of St James on 25 July. At a great ceremony held outside the Capuchins' church, the ruler, after receiving a blessing from the priest, executed two war dances. Then, seated on his throne in the shade of a magnificent tree, he watched while each official, from the captain-general down to the village headmen, first received a blessing from the priest and then executed a war dance, bringing also a symbol of the tribute which they were each obliged to offer the ruler. These ceremonies went on for a fortnight, during which time the missionaries were kept busy dispensing the sacraments of marriage, penance and baptism, Fra Girolamo da Sorrento baptizing 272 people in one day alone.[24] This ancient and well-established festival became matched in Soyo by the feast of St Luke on 18 October, at which the crushing defeat of the Portuguese in 1670 was commemorated with suitable devotion and pride in a crowded and joyous procession.[25] At Mbanza Soyo two of the town's six churches were particularly associated with rulers: one contained the tombs of the rulers and another was the royal chapel.[26] By January 1702 the "Gram Principe de Sonho" had acquired an official seal: the symbolism consisted solely of a cross.[27]

Christian rituals and symbols thus provided an impressive component of the court's pomp and splendour. In these circumstances the excommunication of the ruler became, as

will be seen, a matter of considerable political concern. But
the alliance between missionary and ruler was by no means
limited to their joint participation at Mass. It included an
important element of legitimation by the spiritual powers,
who were intimately concerned with the public ratification
of the ruler's accession. MacGaffey remarks how the can-
didate chief in Kongo "had to submit to inspection by his
peers to ensure that his spirit was appropriate to the role",[28]
and Fra Girolamo describes how, after the election of a ruler
by nine electors, the missionary was immediately informed.
If the choice "had fallen on a worthy individual, the priest
approved it and announced it publicly in church to the populace, otherwise the election would be null and void".[29] The
consent and ritual support of the missionaries was sought
at other crucial occasions: before declaring war the ruler
obtained the approval of the superior of the mission, and
as his army went out to fight it was fortified by Christian
rites.[30] On his side the ruler sent gifts of food to the missionaries and he allocated land to the slaves and servants of the
mission when they married.[31]

The rulers of Soyo may well have had greater need than
the kings of Kongo for the political support and legitimation
provided by Christian rituals. They seem to have lacked a
well-established, indigenous tradition of legitimacy. Dapper's reference in his description of mid-seventeenth century
Soyo to the fact that the area was divided among many
chieftaincies who usually enjoyed independence but who
by that time "lived under another sovereign power",[32]
forcibly suggests the upstart nature of the Soyo ruling establishment as known to the Capuchins. Its fortunes in the
seventeenth century largely rested, as we have seen, on a
series of successful rebellions against San Salvador, followed
by the eventual destruction of this once-powerful capital.
The measure of legitimation bestowed by the new religion
may well, therefore, have been highly valued for political
reasons by the rulers of Soyo.

THE MISSION'S DISCIPLINING OF THE RULING ELITE

Until one can gain a clearer view of the rise of the ruling
dynasty in Soyo, this aspect of the political significance of

Christianity as the source of ritual legitimation must remain somewhat speculative. But it is already abundantly clear that by the last quarter of the seventeenth century the mission had come to occupy a central role in the training, formation and even selection of Soyo's ruling elite. By that time the principal officials gained their education and training during a period of highly disciplined, committed and privileged service in the work of the mission.

The creation of a nucleus of disciplined, committed Christians went back to the early days of the Capuchin mission. Cavazzi describes their bold, "inspired" decision to create congregations or confraternities (brotherhoods) for lay men and women in San Salvador and Mbanza Soyo, as "a stupendous act" taken in the face "of all human reason".[33] The rules of these confraternities insisted that each member should hear Mass daily if at all possible; should make confession and communicate every first and third Sunday in the month taking part in public discipline; should fast every Saturday; should conduct prayers morning and evening and teach their families Christian doctrine; should shun dances and persuade "concubines' to marry.[34] Originally these confraternities were open to all, *Plebei e Nobili*, provided that they were of good reputation. In their early days, at least, they seem to have performed some of the functions of a purification or witchcraft-eradication cult: after the sermon "many would lie prostrate on the ground" voluntarily and publicly confessing their failings.[35] Gradually membership of these confraternities became a prerequisite for high office in Soyo. Already in the early 1660s it was customary for judicial officials to be selected from members of the confraternities,[36] and in 1674 it was reported that the ruler of Soyo was normally selected from among the Confraternity of St Francis.[37]

At the head of this Christian elite were the interpreters or *Maestri della Chiesa*. Eight or ten in number, these men of "noble" birth were, by the end of the seventeenth century, "not only the most cultured in the Land, but also in good part relatives of the Prince".[38] Since few of the Capuchins in late seventeenth-century Soyo had sufficient command of the vernacular, the main task of these interpreters was to assist the missionaries in hearing confessions, and like the priests the interpreters operated under a seal of secrecy. The mission was thus incorporating into its structure the deep desires for purification spontaneously expressed in the early behaviour of members of the confraternities, and by the last quarter of the seventeenth century hand-picked scions of the Soyo rulers, and of the Barreto da Silva patri-lineage in particular, were intimately collaborating in this routinization of piety. The interpreters also prepared the altars and taught "the people the way of Salvation".[39] In return for these services they were relieved of military ser-vice, paid no taxes, enjoyed benefit of clergy in legal cases and were buried with the missionaries. By the 1680s several of the principal officers of the court had served as inter-preters, as had the two rulers elected in the 1690s.[40]

This training, together with membership of the confra-ternities and the obligations which this involved of observ-ing a strict Christian discipline, added an inner, spiritual dimension to the alliance and relationship of missionaries and ruler. It was not simply a question of political necessity or convenient ritual legitimation. Again Cavazzi enables us to catch a glimpse of an early stage in this process. Soon after the formation of the confraternities in the 1640s the ruler of Soyo became suspicious of the activities of these groups and began personally to attend their meetings. In this way he himself became exposed to the detailed teachings of the Capuchins and, under the influence, he repented and decided publicly to adopt Christian marriage.[41] In the relatively scanty evidence which is available it is difficult to trace this thread of inner conviction and to evaluate its influence on the relationship between the missionaries and the rulers; but, as will be seen, it occasionally surfaced, and the early training and service as interpreters and teachers undoubtedly brought missionaries and elite together in an intimate bond of what many of those involved would regard as deep Christian fellowship.

THE TEST-CASE OF CHRISTIAN MARRIAGE

The depth and extent of Christian penetration into Soyo life and culture was, for the Capuchins, measured by their fortunes in two major areas of confrontation. The first was

Christian marriage, as laid down by the Council of Trent. The evidence available suggests that here, somewhat unexpectedly, their efforts at imposing ecclesiastical discipline were being marked with increasing and substantial success. Membership of the Christian elite, the confraternities and the interpreters and teachers, naturally involved an acceptance of canon law marriage. The Capuchins went on to use this example of the ruling elite, together with its political power, to extend this discipline to increasing numbers of the ruler's subjects and dependants. On one occasion, about 1687, when the ruler had been excommunicated, he was ordered as penance to persuade 300 of his subjects to adopt holy matrimony. In the event 400 were presented, and a further 600 immediately followed their example.[42] By that time it was accepted that all the *mani*, the governors and headmen of major towns and villages, should be "legitimately married" or be deprived of their office "lest they should set bad examples to the common people".[43]

Later, at the height of the delicate diplomatic negotiations with the Portuguese, the missionaries decided to launch a further offensive on the matrimonial front. Wishing to train and place teachers in every district to instruct the people and prepare them for Christian marriage, the missionaries gathered the ruler, the electors, the war captains and all the elders into their church, where they pointed out to these leaders the responsibility they had before God towards their subjects, whose "souls were being lost by their negligence". To this appeal the Capuchins added the threat that, if these orders were not promulgated, they would leave and go to other more fruitful fields. Touched probably both by the threat and the appeal, the ruler and his counsellors swore that they wished to live as good Christians, and immediately promulgated the necessary orders. The missionaries and teachers, in company with the ruler or one of the elders, then went out to search for those whom they regarded as living in "concubinage", and in 1689 in Mbanza Soyo alone more than 1000 marriages were celebrated. Three years later the missionaries in Soyo confidently expected that, with the help of a zealous new ruler, Giovanni Barreto da Silva, "soon everyone would be married".[44]

These expectations were wildly over-optimistic, and the

missionaries in general failed totally to appreciate the nature and values of African marriage. Yet the evidence suggests that the principles enunciated in canon law were beginning to become as much respected in Soyo as they were in parts of contemporary Europe, where, as in Soyo, practice often failed to match principle. In the remoter parts of rural Catholic Europe in the eighteenth century, probably a majority of the villagers still lived together without being married according to canon law,[45] so it would hardly have been surprising if among the masses in Soyo the new rules of marriage were often more honoured in the breach than in the observance. Nevertheless the degree to which the missionaries were able to exert presure towards an acceptance of canon law marriage is an extraordinary sign of the extent of their influence on the ruling elite and on the lives of at least those people of Soyo who lived within easy reach of Mbanza Soyo.

THE INTERACTION OF CHRISTIANITY AND INDIGENOUS RELIGION

For the missionaries the other touchstone of Soyo Christianity was the question of the continuing attachment of the people to the shrines, charms and other elements of their religion. The Capuchins' approach was one of straightforward confrontation. Encountering the literate civilizations of Asia some seventeenth-century missionaries had begun to appreciate the necessity of attempting to enter into a dialogue with alien cultures; in tropical Africa, recognition of the values of African institutions and beliefs was to prove far more elusive. Identifying most African rituals as the works of the Devil, the Capuchins generally demanded total renunciation. If a nominal Christian continued impenitently to officiate over these rituals they considered it perfectly just that he or she should be exiled into slavery across the Atlantic.[46] The missionaries assumed that conflict between the new and old religions was inevitable and total. The evidence suggests that some Soyo converts may have agreed with them, and that a few of these were prepared, at least in private, to accept wholeheartedly a radical break with customary beliefs and practices.

While Andrea da Pavia was in Soyo a general assembly of the people was called "with the consent and intervention of the Prince". The question for debate was whether they "wished to observe the laws of God or their superstitious ceremonies". The reply was given that "they firmly believed in God and in everything that was taught them, but that they also believed in their ceremonies and vain observances". Afterwards many came in private to protest against what had been said in public, and these alone were admitted to the sacraments.[47] Besides these committed members of the elite and populace, another group of people who were almost totally identified with the Capuchins were the slaves of the mission, who maintained the hostel, served as medical aides in the hospital,[48] and accompanied the missionaries on their visitations. Shortly after his arrival in Soyo Fra Girolamo found that the slaves of the mission did not hesitate to lay hold of a hostile *nganga*, having no fear of his supernatural powers because they themselves wore medals "given to them by us as preservatives against sorcery".[49]

The hostile *nganga* represented the other extreme of the religious spectrum in Soyo. When Cavazzi visited the area in 1663 he found that there was still a determined resistance against the Christian ruler and his wife. A church had been burnt in Soyo, a hostile charm had been placed against the ruler's wife and guards were mounted in the churches to prevent "some superstitious Christians" from digging up and transporting corpses "into the bush to the graves of their ancestors".[50] By the 1680s, however, the *nganga* in Soyo were very much on the defensive. Fra Girolamo and his confrères led attacks on hidden shrines and the impression is given that traditional ritual experts carried on their practices only at considerable risk to themselves, though, significantly enough, when the missionary and ruler were in dispute over the slave trade, "the magicians and sorcerers" sought to exacerbate the situation.[51]

In between these two extremes of Soyo religious commitment there was, as the reply of the ruler and the general assembly to Fra Andrea indicated, a whole range of people for whom the concept of religious conflict was minimal or even absent. They believed in God and "everything that was taught them", but they also held to their own rituals. For them the new faith was part of a religious spectrum in which they continued to find relevance in many of the old beliefs and practices. Shortly before Fra Girolamo arrived in Soyo the ruler, Antonio II Barreto da Silva, had administered an oath to many of his subjects, some of whom however were able to stage a public protest against this act during Fra Girolamo's first sermon.[52] Antonio II repented that evening, and this eclectic attitude to religion did not generally involve the ruler and people of Soyo in deliberate syncretism, in a conscious attempt to take elements of Christianity and create a new and distinct amalgam of beliefs. In the first decade of the eighteenth century such an attempt did emerge in Kongo around the young, prophetic figure of Dona Beatrice and the Antonine movement, but the people of Soyo, save in the remote south, were hostile to emissaries of this syncretistic sect.[53] In Soyo the interaction between religious beliefs was less dramatic, the process of change being gradual and cumulative.

The situation in Soyo in the late seventeenth century seems to have borne a striking resemblance to that of Kongo in the second half of the twentieth century where as reported by Janzen and MacGaffey, "very few people think of themselves as non-Christian and 'conversion' is no longer an issue".[54] In such a situation most individuals were not continually confronted with stark religious alternatives. There was a large middle ground of "ambivalent flexibility", and across this religious spectrum there was a process of "complex interaction and adaptation".[55] The problem for a historian faced with such a situation is to identify the broad direction of change in religious thought and practice. Of course Christianity was, in Balandier's phrase, "associated with traditional usages", but the crucial question is whether Christianity was being absorbed into an unchanged cosmology, "a system of thought that remains African and traditional rather than European and Christian",[56] or whether the new religion, through its sacraments, liturgy, discipline and literacy, possessed sources of strength which enabled it over time to exert a cumulative impact.

The evidence for late seventeenth-century Soyo suggests,

as we have already seen, that among the ruling elite something of this cumulative influence can be clearly discerned. In this narrow compass, Soyo Christians were constantly being confronted with the challenges presented by the new religion, and many of them were gaining new insights into its implications. For the populace at large the evidence is much less abundant. Here a distinction must be drawn between the situation in Mbanza Soyo with its immediate neighbourhood, and the more distant areas of the region. The influence of the Capuchins was definitely concentrated on the capital. Because of the rains and the pattern of agricultural activity the visits of the missionaries to distant rural areas were restricted to the months from May to September,[57] and even then they could undertake such visits only if there was another priest who could stay behind to maintain the mission at Mbanza Soyo. On their relatively infrequent visits they encountered in rural Soyo an almost universal enthusiasm for baptism, whereas resistance to this rite was encountered in some areas of Kongo. The popularity of baptism indicates a readiness of the majority to accept at least a nominal Christian identification, a move which in the minds of the missionaries exposed these adherents to the dictates of canon law. Baptism by itself could, however, have been readily absorbed by most recipients into an unchanged, folk cosmology. The jubilant acceptance of the rite even in the remoter parts of Soyo may therefore merely have testified to the absence of open hostility to Christian missionaries and their elite assistants.

Confession, however, would seem to be another matter. The rite was by no means a formality: the investigations were often searching and prolonged, while absolution was withheld if the confessor was not convinced that penitence was sincere. Many Capuchin missionaries would have agreed with Fra Giovanni da Romano in regarding the confessional as the principal means of evangelism and of deepening the hold of Christian beliefs and discipline.[58] Like baptism, confession could be seen as essentially a rite of purification and as such highly congruent to Kongo religious practice. Unlike baptism, however, it must have been, at least in most cases, an ordeal not lightly entered upon. Willingness to submit to confession could be a good indication of popular attitudes. When Fra Girolamo visited Kitombo more than a decade after the battle with the Portuguese there, he found that some people had not confessed since then on account of "the great provocation".[59] Among the many hundreds of confessions heard annually by the Capuchins of Soyo some, especially in the outer rural districts, may have been fleeting encounters with little permanent effects, but the readiness of many of the people of Soyo to present themselves for this sacrament, even walking five or six days to do so,[60] would seem to indicate an increasingly wide and deep commitment to the new religion.

Even in folk rituals, a new significance was becoming apparent. The ancestors, for instance, were beginning to be seen as synonymous with the holy souls of Catholic tradition. Fra Andrea da Pavia reported how, after his arrival in Soyo in 1688, he went to bed as usual on the eve of All Souls but was roused almost immediately by many people singing at the top of their voices. Informed by the mission's slaves that this was merely the normal devotions for the dead, he jointed the torch-lit processions which visited the churches in the town and also the cemeteries where the graves were illuminated by many candles. "Everyone was chanting prayers in their language", and Fra Andrea went on to assist them with great enthusiasm. Two hours before daybreak he sounded the church bells, sang the office, celebrated Mass and then led out another procession to the graves where he intoned the responses for the dead. The whole night passed in this manner for sleep was quite impossible. The next day, when all the ceremonies had finished, everyone came with their baskets "each offering alms for the dead", so that the mission distributed ten tons of fruit and other gifts.[61] The sacrifices for the ancestors had become alms for the church's poor; yet, it will be recalled, at the time of Cavazzi's visit only a generation earlier the ruler of Soyo had had to place guards to prevent the reburial of Christians in ancestral cemeteries.

Fra Andrea also glimpsed something of the anguish and dilemma of the majority of Soyo Christians as, faced with the Capuchins' rigid missiology, they attempted to explore and appropriate for themselves these new religious horizons.

When he reported to the Congregation of Propaganda Fide the response of the general assembly called to debate "superstitious ceremonies" (see above), he went on to ask "if in some respects they could be excused, for in their ceremonies they do not make an explicit, or implicit, pact with the Devil, but have a simple faith, from which one tries to raise them as much as one can".[62] His question raised an issue of fundamental missiological significance. His assessment of Soyo rituals in this passage, if not in all his writings, showed far more understanding than that exhibited by most of his confrères, at least in their published works. As he said this was no Devil worship. Indeed he seems to have begun to grasp the fact that their beliefs and rituals represented not only a basic acceptance of supernatural powers but also a continuous attempt to summon their assistance in the constant conflict with evil, however that might be defined. Fra Andrea's final phrase might even imply that he was perhaps ready to take the first vital step towards a recognition of the positive, fundamental values in Soyo religion.

His report was submitted to the Cardinals of Propaganda Fide on 6 April 1693 by Cardinal Gaspare Carpegna, a great canon lawyer. Carpegna was to be an assiduous participant in the Congregation appointed in 1704 to consider the momentous issue of Chinese rites which involved similar missiological problems, so it is interesting to note that a decade earlier he was fairly sympathetic to the problems raised by Fra Andrea. While insisting that "superstitions" should be combated through the confessional, Carpegna went on to suggest that certain sacred rites such as Benediction should be introduced to take the place of "superstitions".[63] The path towards adaptation was not wholly closed, and it might have developed had these Soyo Christians been permitted to foster their own Catholic priesthood. A Capuchin did later advocate the construction of a seminary,[64] but in Soyo the highest post in the church effectively open to local people remained that of interpreter.

THE MISSION, THE RULERS AND THE SLAVE TRADE

This lack of an indigenous priesthood seriously hampered any prospect of a fruitful theological dialogue, and undoubtedly jeopardized the future development of Christianity in Soyo. A more immediate cause of grave tension between the Capuchins and the rulers of Soyo arose from the Atlantic slave trade, which provoked a continued and deepening crisis in the relations of church and state. Acting on a mistaken interpretation of instructions from Propaganda Fide,[65] the Capuchins condemned the sale of baptized slaves to English or other heretical traders. Fra Girolamo twice excommunicated Antonio II, although he himself recognized the dangers of employing this drastic sanction.[66] Some of his successors seem almost to have gloried in their power of interference and their ability to humiliate publicly the rulers of Soyo.[67] Despite the bitter resentment that these theocratic pretensions must have aroused, Antonio III sent a cool, humble petition to Propaganda Fide. Written on 4 October 1701 his letter appealed over the heads of the Capuchins to what he hoped would prove an impartial authority. To the Capuchin insistence that he sold slaves only to the Portuguese or to those Protestants who traded with Catholic ports, the ruler pointed out that the Portuguese would provide him with neither powder nor arms necessary "for our defence against our enemies", and that Protestants trading with Catholic ports were but few in number. Antonio III failed, however, to mention that the trade also supplied him and his court with valued luxury imports, and that strategical considerations were not his sole motive. He, like European Christians involved in the trade, was ensnared in an immense structure of evil. Instead he stressed the necessity of preserving "my Principality and the peace of my People", and he asked permission to conduct this trade without danger of excommunication for "I am a Catholic Prince and desire the accomplishment of my salvation".[68]

The interior, reflective beliefs of individuals are almost totally excluded from the records. Yet as one reads how Antonio III served the mission in his youth rising to the rank of interpreter, and how, despite his sharp disagreements with the Capuchins over the slave trade, he continued "faithfully to promote the apostolate",[69] one is prepared to accept, not as a mere phrase penned by a secretary well trained in ecclesiastical correspondence but as an expression of a deeply held conviction, the claim that he was "a Catholic Prince" and that he desired "the accomplishment of [his] salvation".

CONCLUSION

The records of the late seventeenth century do not therefore depict Christianity in Soyo as affecting "only a slim minority" or as being "weakly established": the judgement of contemporaries might rather have been that it was vigorous, expanding and in some respects almost arrogantly triumphant. One can perceive the ruling institution becomingly increasingly dependent on legitimation by recognized Christian ritual experts; an elite, trained and recruited through exposure to an extremely rigorous religious discipline; a gradual imposition of radically new practices concerning marriage, and the main public festivals becoming centred around the Christian calendar, with the Mass as perhaps the principal ritual focus in Soyo life. One can see Christianity and canon law as features distinguishing Soyo from its northern neighbours. One can even begin to glimpse something of the difficulties and anguish in which the people of Soyo were involved as they explored the implications of this Christian identity, while remaining subject to the jurisdiction of aliens who understood but a small part of this tension and conflict.

In such a situation the cumulative weight of a literate, universal tradition was considerable. The process of religious interaction was dynamic, though its direction could change. Christianity was then, and has ever been, "in constant danger",[70] whether in long-established Christian territories, such as seventeenth-century Italy or France, or on the distant frontiers of overseas missions. Some grounds for deep anxiety had already appeared in Soyo. There was the ominous reluctance to raise an indigenous priesthood. Most obviously there were the tensions arising out of the slave trade, with both European and African Christians enmeshed in the system. With a terrible irony, missionaries and rulers were quarrelling to the point of repeated excommunications over an aspect of this evil whose importance was already, in the considered judgement of the Holy Office as handed down in 1686,[71] paling into insignificance compared with the violation of human rights which the whole system involved. Here indeed the Christian community in Soyo appears as a frail and fragile vessel to confront the greed and cruelty of several continents orchestrated by Europe. The dangers to the Faith were manifold, and these few decades in the late seventeenth century may have constituted for Soyo the deepest point of identification with Christendom. At some subsequent period the impetus slackened, the direction of religious change appears to have altered. One should not, however, allow this later story to determine our assessment of what was happening in the seventeenth century. Church historians should not fall, any more than others, into the trap of Whig interpretations; rather they should recall Ranke's dictum that every generation is equidistant from eternity. The meaning and message of salvation has ever to be discovered anew.

PART TWO

Christians and Colonial Rule;
Syncretism and Orthodoxy

If in the earlier centuries the tiny province of Soyo was something of an exception in the depth of its Christianity, in the modern period the theme of religious interaction already encountered there has been found right across sub-Saharan Africa. One way of explaining the far greater impact of Christian missionaries during the last two centuries is to see them merely as agents of the transformation of Africa by Western capitalism and technology. Missionaries preceded or accompanied traders, soldiers, administrators and settlers so that for many Africans they were indistinguishable from the other aliens who were challenging and changing their values and ways of life. The insistence by many White missionaries on the virtues of regular labour, obedience, individual effort and responsibility neatly fitted the needs of industrial and plantation capitalism, even if their gift of literacy and their control over education enabled a tiny, favoured elite to enjoy some of the benefits of the new era.

All religions are continually in danger of becoming ideologies, and there is much truth in this critical analysis of the White missionaries' role in colonial Africa. This explanation overlooks, however, the complexities of the missionaries' relationships with colonialism. Chapter 4 examines some aspects which distinguished modern missions from other Western forces: their autonomous sources of finance, recruitment and control; their ability to transcend national boundaries, and even at times denominational divisions, and thus to mobilize in Europe and North America an independent critique of colonial policies; the fact that they pioneered African education, often making it impossible for the colonial powers to throttle this process; the range of different contributions that missionaries and the Bible brought to many emergent African challenges to colonial rule. Chapter 4 also considers some of the ways in which church–state relations in both colonial and independent Africa have been moulded by the various experiences of churches in Europe and North America, and it begins to discuss the comparison with the role of Islamic expansion in Black Africa during this modern period. But above all, the argument that Christianity in sub-Saharan Africa has been merely the ideological super-structure of Western capitalism ignores the fundamental con-tributions of African Christians and of African cosmologies.

During the nineteenth and twentieth centuries various aspects of African cosmologies have influenced the develop-ment of Christianity. In the pioneer, pre-colonial period, missionaries were perhaps most conscious of the legitimating role of religion in African polities, of the ways in which religion could support and sustain a political system. African rulers and elders viewed these intruders as agents of Western technology and material influence. Inevitably they also saw them as potential alternative sources of supernatural power. They sought to control this power and influence either by keeping them carefully isolated in separate locations or by incorporating the missionaries and their converts into the ruling structures of the society. The rulers of some of the most powerful African states, the Asante, Dahomey, Zulu and Ndebele kingdoms, viewed the missionaries' claims with suspicion and sometimes hostility. No independent, alter-native source of supernatural power could be tolerated, especially if it was linked in some way with a formidable industrial and military technology. Occasionally such a ruler might make an exception for a particular individual. The mutual friendship and respect of Robert Moffat and Mzili-kazi, ruler of the Ndebele, enabled the London Missionary Society (LMS) to establish a presence in Bulawayo. The activities of the missionaries were, however, severely re-stricted; the number of converts was pitifully small; and, a generation later, in the final crises between the Ndebele and the emissaries of Cecil Rhodes, the missionaries almost without exception sided with the invading settlers. Their ministry had been dwarfed by the material inducements

offered by traders and then by Rhodes, while their message
had been confronted by a resilient religious tradition which
had incorporated the concepts and cults of the western
Shona, conquered earlier by the Ndebele. The missionary
factor in pre-colonial Zimbabwe had been reduced to political insignificance.[1]

Political considerations caused other African rulers to
welcome or tolerate the presence of pioneer missionaries.
Often, as in the case of Kabaka Mutesa, ruler of the powerful
state of Buganda, it was thought that these strangers could
perform a useful function in the field of foreign policy.
Sometimes rulers hoped to enrol their specialist skills for
internal political and developmental purposes. In all cases,
however, the rulers sought to limit or at least control the
spiritual impact of the missionaries. In every instance, even
among the rulers who became Christians, it was thought that
an independent, alien source of supernatural power would
carry a very serious political threat. Moshoeshoe, creator of
the Basuto kingdom, when threatened by the Trekboers
turned to the Paris Evangelical missionaries as an effective
link with the British authorities at the Cape. Yet although
their external political role was of fundamental importance to
his security, and although he was himself influenced by their
teaching and preaching, he rigidly restricted the internal
influence of the missionaries and their converts, consistently
selecting only those aspects of their way of life which, he
thought, could be beneficially incorporated into his kingdom.[2] Even Kgama, ruler of the Ngwato among the northern Tswana, often acclaimed by missionaries as a model
Christian ruler, attempted with a fair degree of success to
control the process of Christianization. Like the princes of
Soyo in the seventeenth century (see above, pp. 42–43),
he sought to make Christianity a dominant legitimating
influence in the political structure. Fertility rites were transformed into national prayers for rain, he downplayed initiation rites, substituted prayers before battle instead of charms
to protect his army and he ended the legal requirement of
bride-price denounced by missionaries. But he refused to
allow the Jesuits to found a station in 1879, saying "they will
cause division among my subjects", and in 1890 he expelled

an LMS missionary who had challenged his authority, reportedly saying "Now the Church is mine. Let all discussion end".[3]

No African ruler, sympathetic or hostile, could ignore the supernatural implications of the arrival of Christian missionaries. Given time, others might have followed in the wake of Kgama and Moshoeshoe in a cool and critical appropriation of the new religion, making their own assessment of its value and benefits, controlling the ability of the missionaries to impose an alien and disruptive set of disciplinary demands. But in the latter half of the nineteenth century, time was not on the side of African rulers. The technological and military superiority of the industrialized powers, the expansive demands of international capitalism, the rivalries of European nations and even their philanthropic concerns all combined to produce a scornful impatience with the independence of African polities. Among the White missionaries the earlier ideals of partnership, of co-operation on an equal footing with Africans, had been overtaken by an aggressive, if often benevolent, paternalism. The qualities of vocation and sacrifice would still distinguish the missionary endeavour. Primarily inspired by love of God and of humanity, young men and, increasingly, women would still leave their homes and families and set out for a continent which in the past had proved more often than not to be a grave for Europeans. But by the last quarter of the nineteenth century most Western missionaries also carried with them the belief that they were representatives of a culture and way of life greatly superior to any that Africa had to offer. As we shall see, as late as 1960, the Dean of the Faculty of Theology at the University of Lovanium in Kinshasa, during a celebrated debate on the possibility of an African theology, maintained that European culture uniquely possessed the "high degree of perfection which the entire world recognizes".[4]

In the early colonial period, therefore, African reactions to Christianity were no longer mainly determined by the traditional African authorities. Increasingly Christianity was being appropriated by the new men, by those who sought the secrets of the conquerors' powers, those who wanted to acquire modern skills and techniques. This was the period when the communities patiently created previously around a mission station suddenly seized the initiative. Before the colonial period, the individuals drawn into these minute, new communities had been restricted in the main to the marginal members of African societies. They had included slaves purchased or protected by the missionaries; barren women; victims of famine or disease; people who had lost their kinsfolk in war or other misfortunates. They had also included a very few enterprising individuals who wanted to acquire the skills brought by the missionaries, or those who were primarily attracted by their teaching and preaching. In the pre-colonial period it had been only the exceptional groups which had grasped Christianity as an essential ingredient of a new identity: the Creoles of Freetown, the Christian revolutionaries in Buganda, or the Tonga by Lake Malawi. All these were societies or groups which fostered the socially mobile, where prestige and influence were determined more by achievement than by birth. Then, in the early colonial period, these early rare examples were imitated on an increasingly massive scale. The marginal outcasts of the mission stations became respected as the intrepid pioneers and interpreters of a new age. This was the golden era of the catechist, the bush-school teacher, the clerk and literate boss-boy. This was the period when it suddenly seemed that the Creoles, Ganda, Tonga and others had stolen a march on most African societies.

This was the period when it seemed that White missionaries would be most influential in the development of African Christianity. For a while it seemed to them that tropical Africa at last lay open before them and that they had been granted a unique opportunity. When the young Lavigerie, the future founder of the White Fathers, one of the most influential missionary societies to be created specifically for Africa, accepted the See of Algiers in 1867 he already saw his archdiocese as "a door opened by Providence on a barbarous continent of 200 million souls. There is the great prospect which attracts me. Would you find in France a task more worthy to tempt the heart of a bishop? Would you even find a similar task?".[5] Like Erasmus three centuries earlier, he saw Africa as a *tabula rasa* waiting before him, though the missionary society which Lavigerie founded was later notable for a recognition of the need to respect indigenous cultures.

Almost simultaneously with this White triumphalism, African reactions began to be marked by disappointment and delusions. The new men, those few who, often at considerable cost, had acquired the new skills and had even successfully acquired the same academic qualifications as their White teachers and rulers, discovered that this long, laborious apprenticeship had not opened for them the way into the charmed circle of power and influence. The Gospel might proclaim that God was no respecter of persons, but His European servants were deeply conscious of racial and class differentials. The whole structure of colonial rule rested on the seemingly inviolable prestige of the Whites. And beyond the few Africans who so laboriously reached even the lowest rungs of the educational ladder, stood the mass of villagers, old and young, women and men, increasingly desirous of putting the new religion to the test, wanting, sometimes desperately wanting, to discover whether these new rituals, this new mode of communication with the supernatural, would provide them with effective access to a power which could solve both their age-old problems of disease, poverty and social control, and also assist them in the harsh new trials which colonialism brought in its wake. The vast majority of White missionaries resolutely barred the way to mass baptisms. The gate into the new community was straight and narrow. Generally it involved the acquisition of literacy; always it demanded the acceptance of a perplexing plethora of disciplinary restrictions, often apparently diametrically opposed to previous marriage and kinship customs and beliefs.

Yet in the midst of this disillusion and despair, authentic African appropriations of Christianity were developing. This is the key to African church history in the twentieth century. This is the process which has produced much of the contemporary vitality of African Christianity. This is the matrix out of which the distinctive African contributions to the universal church are being made.

The most dramatic instances of this process of appropriation have often been the challenges posed to the mission-connected churches by the Ethiopian churches in Southern and West Africa, by the great prophetic figures like Shembe, Harris and Kimbangu, and by the thousands of independent Christian healers and leaders (see below, pp. 99, 103). Understandably, much scholarly attention has been focused on them. But within the mission churches, Africans of all ages and classes were constantly attempting to reconcile the new religion with their inherited insights and traditions. Even at the moment of greatest missionary influence, vital spaces remained open for African initiatives and responses. The denominational and other rivalries between the various Western missions did much to temper the tendencies and practices of theocratic absolutism. Even more important was the fact that the rapidity and scale of African responses to Christianity succeeded in reducing the personal influence and impact of the Whites to an acceptable minimum. Many African Christians had but the briefest of exposures to a White missionary.

Even those Africans closest to White missionaries often retained a remarkable independence. Take for instance the case of Alfred Diban. Rescued as a young man by the White Fathers on the upper Niger while escaping from a slave trader, Diban was subsequently one of their most faithful and energetic assistants in planting the Catholic Church in Upper Volta. He was an outstanding exemplar of the ardour, courage and rectitude of a pioneer convert. Yet as one reads the testimonies carefully collected by his son, the historian Joseph Ki-Zerbo, one becomes aware that, despite the enormous debt Diban owed to the teaching and discipline of his French fathers in God, he suffered little or no sense of a traumatic culture shock, and that there was in his life plenty of room for vital continuities with the past. Even though a new community which transcended old kinship ties was created around him, the new group looked to this man of prayer for defence and healing, two of the essential functions of traditional religious leaders among his people.[6] If for this man, who willingly accepted total obedience to missionary discipline and direction, there yet remained room for a spontaneous, distinctively African spirituality to emerge, how much greater was the scope for these independent initiatives and contributions within the mission-connected churches out in the bush and in the shanty towns.

An essential task in any assessment of contemporary Christianity in Africa is to examine the nature and influence of these specifically African contributions, this input into world Christianity which has been moulded by particular African traditions and experiences. We know all too little about the membership and organization of the myriad small, local Christian communities. A workshop held by the Association of Theological Institutions in Southern and Central Africa has underlined the urgent necessity of collecting data on the life and spirituality of these communities. It is hoped that this Association and other similar bodies will mobilize students and church persons to gather this data, and then to analyse and discuss it in seminars and in a wider forum.[7]

One of the most sophisticated and influential attempts to examine some of these implications has been that of Robin Horton.[8] Placing almost the whole of his emphasis on the potential of change within African religions, Horton has argued that what had seemed to be perhaps the most dramatic element in African conversion to Christianity – the replacement of the old spirits and gods by the belief in the High God – should now be seen primarily as a logical response of traditional religion to the expansion of scale, to the transformation of the narrow, local viewpoints of small communities by the wider horizons brought to Africa by the revolution in communications. Indeed, in Horton's scheme, the world religions of Christianity and Islam are very nearly reduced "to the role of catalysts – i.e. stimulators and accelerators of changes which were 'in the air' anyway".[9] This is not the occasion to question the strengths of Horton's particular argument concerning the place of the High God vis-à-vis the local spirits,[10] but a historian, whether or not he belongs to what Horton terms "the devout opposition",[11] is likely to suspect any thesis that claims to provide "an overall causal explanation"[12] of a phenomenon as complex as conversion in Africa. We are deeply indebted to Horton for his decisive demonstration of the need to investigate the dynamics of religious change in Africa, but his approach would seem to overlook the possibility that the world religions may have introduced completely new concepts to the African religious repertory. By querying one of his initial assumptions and by concentrating on one or two of his more questionable assertions, we would seek to direct attention to some rather neglected aspects of the debate on the still developing process of Christianization in Africa. Is it, for instance, correct to assume that increased attention to the High God is the most notable feature of African responses to Christianity?

One of the most obvious aspects of African encounters with Christianity has involved beliefs concerning life after death. John Mbiti's study[13] is justly well known but it is surprising how few other scholars have followed his lead,[14] and that the relevance of eschatology to the debate on conversion has largely been overlooked. Yet, even the most superficial survey of missionary literature will produce illustrations of the impact of Christian eschatology on African cosmologies and on the imagination of African individuals.

Some anthropologists have emphasized the fear and horror which death held for some African peoples:

> Nuer avoid as far as possible speaking of death and when they have to do so they speak about it in such a way as to leave no doubt that they regard it as the most dreadful of all dreadful things. This horror of death fits in with their almost total lack of eschatology. Theirs is a this-worldly religion, a religion of abundant life and the fullness of days, and they neither pretend to know, nor, I think, do they care, what happens to them after death.[15]

This fear and horror, however, should be placed in perspective by the successful balance achieved by most African societies in their relationship to the ancestors, so that in traditional Africa death was often seen as an opportunity to strengthen life.[16] But whether death was viewed with horror or accepted triumphantly, there was a relative paucity in African cosmologies of speculations concerning the nature of life after death. And even where there were fairly clear ideas about the after life, where the village of the ancestors was seen as a highly desirable "continuation of life on earth without any of the worries, trouble or afflictions that mar this world", the enjoyment by the soul of this future life was recognized to be extremely tenuous, dependent as it was on the periodic acts of remembrance by its descendants at ancestral shrines. The probable final end of man was thus to pass into the collective obscurity of forgotten spirits.[17]

The insistence of the Christian catechism on "the fear of hell and the beauty of heaven", the two aspects most emphasized, for instance, in the Ganda catechism of 1881,[18] was reinforced by the confessional, where impenitents could again be reminded of the pains of hell.[19] It was reiterated in much early missionary preaching, and was proclaimed, perhaps most cogently, by the calm heroic deaths of so many pioneer missionaries. All this presented an immense challenge to most African peoples. Often, as Mbiti argues, the Christian eschatological symbolism has been presented in such a way that it has been interpreted at a literal level inducing a psychological escape to a dream land,[20] and the prevalence of millenarian expectations among the first generation of Christian converts has been widely recognized.[21]

Yet, even where African reactions have not taken millenarian forms, the evidence suggests that the impact of Christian eschatology has been widespread and profound. We are told, for instance, that among Ganda Catholics "prayers to and for the dead and the baptizing of the dying to assure them of heaven, had a great appeal to the converts".[22] A young Alur chief, Okelo of Panyamure, noted by a pioneer Verona Father as the area's most assiduous catechumen, explained his motives as follows: "my father is dead and I do not know where he is now; but I, when I die, want to go to heaven";[23] and an early CMS missionary remarked in Buganda that "the idea of everlasting life appeals to them, their life here being so uncertain".[24] It is notoriously difficult for a historian to identify religous motivations, especially when he is dependent largely on the reports of alien observers. Yet these impressions of the importance of Christian eschatology are powerfully reinforced by the evidence of at least one social anthropologist. "Again and again we were told by Christians: 'We do not fear death as the pagans do'," reports Monica Wilson of her experiences among the Nyakyusa in the 1930s. "The supreme attraction, mentioned again and again as the reason for conversion, is: 'There is life' (*ubumi bulipo*), and it is life in a world to come rather than 'more abundant life' here and now that is spoken of".[25] The later theological emphasis on realized eschatology had not apparently influenced these early converts. The appeal and impact of early missionary teaching rested, therefore, not merely on the changes and chances of this mortal life but on the fact that it involved a cosmological revolution. Suddenly the hereafter was no longer a faint reflection of this world, no longer was it primarily concerned with the community's survival, no longer would it slip imperceptibly into the forgotten past. The Bible brought to its African readers the idea of history as progress,[26] the concept of linear rather than cyclical time, and with this was linked a liberating yet frightening emphasis on the individual.[27]

Many other factors have, of course, heightened the emphasis on the ego,[28] and it would be quite false to suggest that African responses to Christian eschatology have been taking place in a vacuum, that they have not been accompanied and affected by many other social and economic factors, still less that they have been confined to the narrow orthodox ranks of Christian "converts".[29] But when examining this major transformation of ideas in Africa it is difficult to believe that these African responses were "in the air" anyway. Rather, it would seem that Christian eschatology was almost completely unexpected and that its introduction in areas unaffected by Islam posed a fundamentally novel, and in some ways perhaps a decisive, challenge to the cosmologies of many African peoples.

The final chapter in this book suggests another way in which the messages brought by missionaries have interacted with deeply entrenched African cosmologies, with their concerns, interests and fears. We have seen that some Africans valued the missionary contribution because it helped them to master the process of modernization and to survive the challenges of colonialism (see above p. 62 and below p. 97). A few of these educated Africans saw the Kingdom of Heaven in terms of overcoming the evils of racial discrimination and political oppression, and this particular appropriation of

Christianity powerfully fostered many elements in African nationalisms. But beyond the educated few have stood the masses, and they have often seen Christianity as immensely relevant to a very different face of evil: the sufferings associated with disease, poverty and death and also the misfortunes inherent in human experience. They have seen in the Christ of the Gospels and in the work of the Holy Spirit a source of healing and salvation here and now. Can Christian symbols, faith and rituals enable these two strands, these two concepts of evil, to combine and produce an effective synthesis, a prophetic vision of liberation of vital relevance to Africa but also to the world in general? Chapter 5 suggests some ways in which this synthesis, this African input and contribution, is already taking shape.

Some observers of Christianity in Africa maintain, however, that such a synthesis carries with it the dangers of syncretism. During the session on African religions at the Sixteenth International Congress of Historical Sciences at Stuttgart in 1985, historians from East Germany and the Soviet Union insisted on applying the term syncretism to the process of religious development in Africa. Perhaps this is because some Marxists, like certain missionaries, are confident that all the aspects of orthodoxy can be established with clarity and finality.[30] In general usage, religious syncretism is understood as seeking to create a new religious system with beliefs and practices drawn from two or more religions. Some twenty years ago, John Peel argued that such syncretism should be carefully distinguished from other forms of religious change among the Yoruba in West Africa: "A syncretist," he wrote, "is a man who sees some good, as many Yorubas have done, in his traditional religious practices and beliefs, identified as such, and attempts to synthesize them with new beliefs in a harmonious religious system".[31]

In this sense of attempting to create a new religion, Yoruba syncretists regard Orunmila, the god of divination, as God's prophet for Africa. Elsewhere in Nigeria, Olumba Olumba Obu, the Sole Spiritual Leader of the Brotherhood of the Cross and Star, the largest and best known of all the indigenous religious movements in Calabar, is regarded as "the second reincarnation of Christ, the personification of the Holy Spirit, and even God himself".[32] Another example of syncretism could be taken from Zimbabwe, where the Guta ra Jehovah (City of God) movement led by Mai Chaza has "deliberately replaced the Bible with a revelational book of its own . . . with Mai Chaza elevated to one of the three divine Persons who was present even during the creation".[33]

These are examples of conscious, deliberate syncretism. But is there a much wider, perhaps more insidious type of syncretism? An ongoing study of some lyrics composed and sung by Yoruba Christians suggests that the authors of these lyrics reveal "a certain amount of confusion as they try to reconcile two opposing sets of beliefs in an inconsistent manner". One song, for instance, in attempting to proclaim a firm Christian faith, also draws on Yoruba concepts of reincarnation and asserts that "if I come to this world again, I will be a believer". Benjamin Oyetade predicts that the author and the singers would deny any contradiction for "they are unaware of the mingling of the beliefs in question", and he suggests that this is "syncretism beyond the level of consciousness".[34] Is Africa likely to drift into becoming a post-Christian continent, with many people accepting a variety of mixtures of beliefs and practices? Will these gradually harden into syntheses which Christians in Africa and elsewhere will be forced to reject as worse than dangerous and misleading heresies?

Some Christians in Africa are deeply perturbed by the gravity of this threat. Byang Kato, the young Nigerian whose early death in 1975 deprived the Association of Evangelicals of Africa and Madagascar of a distinguished representative, was in no doubt of its seriousness. "The spirit of syncretism in Africa," he proclaimed, "is predominant today both inside and outside church circles".[35] Another writer deeply influenced by Karl Barth's antithesis between the Revelation of God and the magic circle of religion is G.C. Oosthuizen. In his survey of "so-called separatist or indigenous movements in sub-Saharan Africa", he suggests that "many form easy bridges back to nativism. They are neither Christian nor traditional, but a syncretism of both, and thus a new religion". The process of mixing "by people who stand in the old and select from the new, leads to syncretism pure and simple".[36]

Among Catholics, the debate concerning syncretism in Africa has been focused on the possibility of developing indigenous theologies. Most missionaries trained in the scholasticism of the first half of the twentieth century found it difficult to accept the legitimacy or even the feasibility of an African theology. This was true even of some of the most intelligent and sympathetic missionaries. One of my most vivid recollections of the seminar on Christianity in Tropical Africa, organized by the International African Institute and held at Legon in 1965, was of René Bureau, fresh from presenting his brilliant, if Eurocentric, analysis of the impact of Christianity on the Duala, vehemently disputing with the Zaïrean, Vincent Mulago, the possibility of an African theology. "Theology," Bureau maintained, "was a universal science, and one could not contrast African with Western theology". We were all increasingly part of a universal, technological civilization founded on Jewish thought and Greek ideas, and another Western missionary maintained "it was as unreal to talk of an African theology as of a lay theology".[37]

The principal battlefield was the newly founded Faculty of Theology at the University of Lovanium. Here in January 1960 a debate took place between T. Tshibangu, then still a student but subsequently to become auxiliary Bishop of Kinshasa and rector of the National University, and A. Vanneste, Dean of the Faculty. Against Tshibangu's plea for a recognition of the way in which specific inputs from African cultures and viewpoints could lead to a "théologie de couleur africaine", Vanneste insisted on the universal characteristics of "une vraie théologie", constructed from a patient examination of the sources of revelation, an examination which remained in permanent contact with "the great currents of universal thought". Questioning the value of an appeal to popular wisdom and the attempt to integrate "certain elements of African tradition" into a theological system, Vanneste went on to make the remark quoted earlier concerning the perfection of European culture.[38] Orthodoxy was seen as an almost static corpus of belief; innovations or insights introduced from outside the solid core of Western thought and experience were irrelevant, or worse they smacked of syncretism.

Thus some theologians surveying developments both in the Catholic Church and in the Independent Churches have been, and still are, apprehensive. They fear that the desire to question and to reject much that many Western missionaries have felt to be central to Christian faith and practice will lead to disaster. Like the Marxists at the Stuttgart conference, they perceive abundant evidence in Africa of syncretism, be it open and conscious, or hidden and therefore even more insidious.

Against these fears must be set a confidence born of ecumenical encounters. The classic and most powerful demonstration of this process in an African context is to be found in the work of Bengt Sundkler. His *Bantu Prophets in South Africa* was the first attempt to present sympathetic, rounded accounts of the founders, leaders and members of African Independent churches. Rapidly his book was recognized as having opened a new horizon in African studies. But at that time, as he made clear in his inaugural lecture at Uppsala in 1949, Sundkler was still deeply concerned with the dangers of syncretism,[39] and in *Bantu Prophets* he concluded that "the syncretistic sect becomes the bridge over which Africans are brought back to heathenism".[40] His research had, however, been based on deep personal encounters. Some forty years later, a Zulu woman was to recall vividly to another great Swedish Africanist, Axel-Ivar Berglund, the nature of these early encounters. A member of Sundkler's parish, she had been healed from barrenness by accepting a prophet's baptism in a ceremony witnessed by Sundkler. Fearing his reproach, she avoided him until one day she met him on a country path. Gently he questioned her, seeking to understand

what had taken place there at the waterfall in the pool. . . . It was not before the sun began casting long shadows that we parted, taking leave of one another, both as worthy human beings. I tell you, he amazed me very much. For he neither scolded nor dismissed. We shared as if we were of the same family, speaking nicely to one another without any bad words.[41]

The understanding and impetus born of such ecumenical encounters was to mature steadily,[42] until in *Zulu Zion* Sundkler acknowledged that

> to those in the movement, Zion meant newness of life, health and wholeness, a new identity. If it was a bridge, it appeared to them as a bridge to the future . . . the intention of the Zulu prophet was to establish a new, Christian community. . . . From his point of view he had taken an infinitely decisive and radical step, away from the Past, baptized to the new life, walking henceforth towards the New Land.[43]

Another writer whose earlier suspicions of syncretism in Africa have been radically revised is Marie-Louise Martin. In a dissertation of 1964 based mainly on accounts of prophetic movements published by outside observers, Martin had dismissed the Kimbanguist Church of Zaïre, together with certain South African movements, as messianic. Christ, she thought, was overshadowed and even replaced by Simon Kimbangu. Active participation in the life and worship of the Kimbanguists transformed her, however, into an ardent apologist and leading theologian of the Church.[44] One can discern here a pilgrimage by an outsider, who, with joyful and in some respects humble surprise, came to recognize a Christian identity and spirituality within the Kimbanguist Church, and in the process deepened and widened her own understanding of Christianity.

A recent study of the theology expressed in Kimbanguist hymns has suggested that two theological currents coexist within the Kimbanguist church. One is Christo-centric; the other much less so. From the point of view of a Kimbanguist, however, it should not be assumed that

> the two are incompatible in such a way as to compel him to belong either to a so-called non-official, Kimbangu-centric majority or to a so-called Christo-centric reformist circle of the present leaders. . . . On the contrary, the two perceptions are co-existing and "organically related" and

the Kimbanguist finds it quite possible to be able to slip, as the need arises, from one perception to the other and back again.[45]

Theological pluralism of the type exemplified by these Kimbanguists is, surely, a more accurate model than syncretism of much religious development in Africa. It implies a continuous process of dialogue. It is perhaps the dominant characteristic of contemporary Christianity in Africa. It is quite distinct from the deliberate mixing of Christianity and indigenous beliefs in order to create a new, specifically African religion, because this process of dialogue takes place among those who claim to be Christian. Syncretism, if it ceases to be unconscious, must by definition result in the creation of a recognizably "unorthodox" religious belief or practice. But theological pluralism, if and when it is resolved, may lead to theological enrichment. Admittedly such pluralism can exist only in situations where it is not immediately imperative to define rigid boundaries. But this surely is the position that most people find themselves in for most of the time. Even those pioneer missionaries who came from alien cultures could not be continually obsessed by conflict; even the most aggressive had to search for bridges, had to enter into some form of dialogue, be it of the most elementary and tenuous nature.

Theological pluralism is partly, as many anthropologists emphasize, an indication of the continuing strength and vitality of African cultures. This is so much the case that some people have concluded that most Africans who claim to be Christians have merely adopted a few Christian rituals and practices while their basic cosmology has remained unchanged. A Christian veneer has been superimposed on old religious forms. Some people believe that institutional and other modernizing inducements have been responsible for the massive numerical growth of Christianity in Africa. If these factors are removed, this religion will be revealed as a fragile, alien, superfluous and temporary aberration.

A recognition of the vitality of African cultures need not, however, lead to such a conclusion. Chapter 5 argues that Africans' tolerance of religious diversity has provided many opportunities for a fruitful, cumulative interaction between the Bible and the sacraments brought by missionaries on the one hand and indigenous concepts and concerns on the other. Theological pluralism is not a rigid, still less a static, phenomenon. It is flexible, but also resilient. The boundaries of thought and practice are open to change and to development.

Should one, however, assume that this movement of religious change, this cumulative impact, is directed towards an established understanding of orthodoxy? The experience of Sundkler and Martin suggests that Christians from a rigid, Western tradition can be brought by African Christians into a broader and deeper recognition of Christianity. This is also the implication of an acceptance of the legitimacy of African theologies, an acceptance mightily strengthened by Vatican II and enshrined in papal pronouncements, however much this acceptance has still to be worked out in practice. For one of the essential consequences of the acceptance of the possibility of African theologies is that Africans are given responsibility for the faith, and that they take the inevitable risks associated with such responsibility. As Father Hebga, the Camerounian theologian, has asserted:

> Undoubtedly we will make mistakes and errors. They will not be worse than those of the East and those of the West, and we will bear in mind their long experience. The European or American churches who are known to be without fault, will cast on us the first stone.[46]

We must reconsider the meaning of orthodoxy, or at the very least what it means to claim a Christian identity. Stephen Sykes has argued that Christianity is, and has always been, "an essentially contested concept . . . the contestants are held together by the conviction that the contest has a single origin in a single, albeit internally complex, performance". Anyone can participate in this contest, in this argumentative search for understanding, who accepts the basic definition of a Christian as "one who gives attention to Jesus whose achievement is contextualized by God". This definition in no way seeks to give an adequate description of the substance or quality of a disciple's attention to Jesus. It does not define orthodoxy. It merely indicates the area in which the contests occur, the never-ending process of defining orthodoxy. Even if the contestants do not agree about the rules of the game, for example concerning the nature of biblical authority, they can still participate in it. "Christianity only becomes interesting as a concept when someone has the courage to spell out in greater or lesser detail one or other of the contestable possibilities which the definition permits".[47]

There is nothing static about orthodoxy, and one of the most powerful influences for theological development has always been the encounter with different cultures. Owen Chadwick has reminded us that Newman perceived the assimilative power of Christianity as it moved out into the Jewish dispersion among the Greeks:

> It has to commend its gospel in a society where intelligent men use the language of Greek philosophy, Platonic or Stoic. Its missionaries start to talk that language, then to think in that language. This is a very sure way of throwing up what, very early, the Church called "heresy", that is, ways of expressing the gospel which were felt to be unfaithful to the authentic gospel: an attempt which tried and failed to express the truth. But it also gave the Christians a lot of new insights and modes of expression which were felt to be authentic. . . . Newman had a conviction about this strength in Christian thought to assimilate all that was right and good in the thought of the non-Christian world.[48]

From such an understanding of orthodoxy, it is necessary to challenge the adequacy of a concept of conversion which demands a sudden, sharp break: "an old spiritual home was left for a new once and for all". There was a consciousness "that a great change is involved, that the old was wrong and the new is right".[49] We may of course agree tht conversion can sometimes involve a sudden, total acceptance of a Gospel which appears to the convert to demand a radical, almost complete reorientation of life. African responses to Christianity have indeed included examples of such revolutionary religious change.[50] The blood of the martyrs has been and still is the seed of the church in many known, and in many unrecorded, cases. But perhaps even more than in late antiquity or in Europe, the growth of Christianity in sub-Saharan

Africa has also been the result of a far more open, piecemeal process of religious reorientation. In Black Africa conversion has drawn deeply on the springs of toleration, humility and wisdom inherent in Africans' age-old searchings for truth and salvation. This mode of conversion is one in which African responses to Christianity have involved not only examples of sudden, radical change, and of obedience to missionary teachings, but also a much more temperate, prolonged dialogue in which the universal church's understanding of orthodoxy is itself modified, developed and enriched. As a result of this experience of toleration we may hope that Africa will be spared the horrors which have flowed elsewhere from the springs of religious fanaticism, pride and blindness; though, as one writes, the omens do not appear to be particularly promising, especially in those areas, such as the Sudan and Nigeria, where the two main inheritors of the Judaic tradition confront each other.

CHAPTER 4

Christianity, Colonialism and Communications[1]

For nearly a thousand years Islam was by far the more significant of the two world religions that have deeply influenced
tropical Africa. It has been estimated, however, that since the
mid-nineteenth century the number of Africans who claim a
Christian identity has been doubling about every twelve
years. If this trend continues, there may well be 350 million
Christians in Africa before 2000 AD.[2] And this change is not
merely a question of numbers. In 1870, apart from the
ancient kingdom of Ethiopia and the settlements of Sierra
Leone, Liberia and South Africa, Christians were an insignificant minority in nearly all sub-Saharan societies. By 1970
Christianity had become the dominant religious influence
among many African societies, and the social and political
influence exerted by African Christians far exceeded that
warranted merely by their numbers. During this period of
unprecedented social and cultural change, at least until the
early 1970s, it was Christianity rather than Islam that had
made the greatest impact south of the Sahara.

CHRISTIANITY AND COLONIALISM

Like most generalizations dealing with so vast an area, this
assertion concerning the comparative growth of Christianity
and Islam undoubtedly requires many qualifications. But it
also demands an explanation. Many observers would assume
that the reason is fairly self-evident. The century 1870–1970
roughly coincided with the colonial period and its immediate
aftermath. Christianity, it is argued, made its rapid advances
precisely because its emissaries, the missionaries, were so
closely linked with the whole apparatus of colonial rule.

This is an attractive thesis. Undoubtedly these links were close. For a variety of reasons many missionaries advocated imperial expansion during the latter part of the nineteenth century. Indeed, the principal aspect of this story debated among historians is whether this missionary advocacy effectively influenced the partition of Africa or whether the missions were merely manipulated by European statesmen for their own secular aims and ambitions.[3] In the twentieth century most missionaries co-operated with the colonial regimes, even if on occasions they criticized some colonial policies, with varying degrees of effectiveness. As the work of many African novelists has illustrated, for many Africans there was little if any difference between an administrator and a missionary.

BLACK CHRISTIAN INITIATIVES

This explanation of the influence of Christianity in Africa overlooks, however, three fundamental considerations. In the first place, it incorrectly identifies Christianity in Africa with the Western missionary. It also ignores the extent to which the missions were able independently to initiate the modern communications revolution in Black Africa and, thirdly, it overlooks the ways in which this revolution has been intimately associated with Christian cosmology.

The whole thrust to recent research on this subject has exposed the extent to which the growth, expansion, and development of Christianity south of the Sahara has depended on, and been distinctively moulded by, African initiatives. This is most obvious in the case of those African churches that have separated from the missions or were founded independently. The prophets and ministers who led thousands of Africans into these movements were manifestly proclaiming that, for them, Christianity was no longer an alien intrusion but a faith that had become indigenous. The same process of indigenization can be clearly discerned within the mission-connected churches. Right from the start the expansion of Christianity in West Africa depended largely on Blacks. It was the Nova Scotian settlers of African descent who ensured that Freetown developed a distinctive

Christian culture and who provided the reference group for the colonies of freed slaves.[4] It was these Sierra Leoneans who as ministers, teachers and traders were the pioneer evangelists in southern Nigeria and the neighboring areas.[5] In the Gold Coast the first Methodist missionaries were originally summoned to the area by Fante Christians, while the Presbyterian church, founded by Basle and West Indian missionaries, soon developed an indigenous leadership which by World War I was strong enough to seize and retain control of the church's affairs.[6] In the interior of Africa south of the equator, although most of the pioneer mission stations were founded by Whites, it was African catechists, teachers, traders and migrant labourers who assimilated the faith and initiated villagers, kinsfolk, workmates and strangers into this new identity.[7]

ENCOUNTER WITH AFRICAN BELIEFS

African initiatives were not restricted to the work of these pioneer evangelists. The encounter between Christianity and indigenous beliefs, rituals and customs involved a massive and continuous process of interpretation and reassessment. The traditional concerns, hopes and fears of many Africans, often ignored or belittled by missionaries from an alien culture, asserted their claims on the new religion. Often, especially at first, this involved a distortion or misunderstanding of the nature of Christian teachings. In these cases the beliefs and symbols of the world religions were merely absorbed and taken over by the indigenous religions, which were themselves developing in response to social change.[8] But the interacion was a dynamic two-way process. The long-term, cumulative advantage lay with the world religions with their sacred writings, literacy, large-scale organization, and universalist claims,[9] but in meeting African needs, both Christianity and Islam adopted new characteristics, discovered new insights, and themselves became indigenous.

This encounter assumed innumerable forms. One of its most dramatic aspects concerned the problem of evil, which for most Africans was most sharply represented by negative spiritual forces. The sins of anger, lust, envy, pride and hatred were often personified in the activities of sorcerers and witches. At first the proclamation of Christ's salvation was interpreted by many African communities as implying the dramatic arrival of a spiritual power akin to the series of beneficent spirits, who, with their charms and shrines, had previously claimed to cleanse the community from the evil of witchcraft.[10] Sometimes this saving aspect of "Christianity" assumed drastic and horrendous forms. In 1925 Tomo Nyirenda, who had been influenced by the millenarianism of Jehovah's Witnesses, embarked upon a career of identifying and slaughtering witches, but to the Lala people in Zambia he appeared as "before all else the bearer of Christianity . . . a Mission like any other".[11] Here the Christian message of salvation was being interpreted in terms almost exclusively determined by traditional concepts, but later generations of Christians substantially modified their approach to the task of witchcraft eradication. Thirty years after Nyirenda, Alice Lenshina in Zambia sought to cleanse her Lumpa church from fears of witchcraft through baptism, prayer and praise, and a similar transformation has been reported among the Xhosa in South Africa, where the reliance of Christians on prayer rather than on traditional diviners has assisted in a radical decline of specific accusations of witchcraft with their traumatic social consequences.[12]

Here, then, one can begin to perceive how successive generations of African Christians have brought Christianity into contact with traditional cosmologies, and how in this encounter Africans have helped the Christian churches to develop an effective concern with beliefs and phenomena that modern Western missionaries had been inclined to ignore. The same process occurred in another dimension of traditional belief. The incidence of sickness and infertility led Africans not merely to seek to eradicate witchcraft but also for positive spiritual assistance, to have recourse to possession cults and other forms of spiritual healing. When African Christians began to read the New Testament they discovered that Christ and the Apostles had also been heavily involved in spiritual healing. By the end of the nineteenth century most Western missionaries were emphasizing, and some were bringing, the benefits of medical science, but in a few

cases Africans established direct links with those Pentecostalists, who in North America and Europe were, at that very
moment, renewing Western concern in the ministry of
spiritual healing. In other cases, the links with Pentecostalists
in the West were far more tenuous, but they helped to emphasize the universal significance of this African response to
the Bible.[13] The links with Western Pentecostalism seem,
however, to have been non-existent in some of the most
spectacular African responses, as for example in the career
and impact of the prophets William Wade Harris and Simon
Kimbangu. The message and influence of these two men,
which resulted in the formation of large Christian communities along the West African coast and in Zaïre,[14] illustrate the
extent to which the call to purification and healing emerged
almost automatically as a dominant aspect of the Gospel in
Africa. Indeed the significance of African understandings of
the relevance of spiritual factors in most healing processes
was, of course, by no means limited to the prophets or
members of Independent churches. Within the mission-
connected churches, especially at local, grassroots or shanty-
town levels, Africans of all Christian denominations eagerly
seized on the relevance of biblical healing accounts. They
realized, even if many of the White missionaries seemed to
have forgotten, that healing very often involves social,
emotional and deeply spiritual dimensions.[15] Here African
Christianity is proclaiming a Christian belief with universal
relevance; indeed it is challenging that emphasis on technology which, as we shall see, has been so beloved in recent
centuries by the West.

The reaction to fears of witchcraft and the ministry of
healing are merely two ways in which the development of
Christianity in sub-Saharan Africa since 1870 has depended
not on alien intruders but on indigenous enterprise. Any
assessment of the connections between Christianity and
colonialism must therefore surely begin by recalling this
basic fact. African Christianity is not the result primarily of a
massive campaign of brainwashing by foreign missionaries.
Whatever the missionaries may have thought, Africa was no
tabula rasa. Aspects of Christianity were eagerly accepted and
transformed by Africans because this faith was seen to meet

not merely the exigencies of modernization but also at least some of the longstanding spiritual needs and demands of African societies. Christianity in Africa was never synonymous with the missionaries' understanding of the faith; the encounter with Africa involved a process of interaction in which Africa's distinctive characteristics and contributions have become ever increasingly prominent.

MODERNIZATION

The vital dimension of African initiatives does not, however, explain by itself the rapidity of Christianity's recent growth in sub-Saharan Africa. It reveals the fallacy of equating this phenomenon with alien missionary activity or the mere influence of colonial rule, but it hardly illuminates the comparison with Islam. For in the century under consideration, the growth and expansion of Islam in Africa was, to an even greater extent than Christianity, the product of African rather than alien initiatives, and the encounter between Islam and Black African societies involved at least as great a segment of indigenous beliefs. Africans found in Islam, just as much as in Christianity, a source of spiritual assistance when confronted with the problems of evil and suffering. Like Christianity, Islam also brought to Black Africa a more vivid and complete picture of life after death than that possessed by most indigenous cosmologies.[16] It is only when one turns to consider the process of modernization, the comprehensive nature of recent social change in Africa, and the contribution of the revolution in communications, that the contrast between the modern roles of Christianity and Islam begins to assume significance.

In order to appreciate the precise contribution of Christianity to modernization in Africa, it is necessary to take up again the question of the relationship of the missions to the colonial powers. We have already noted that for many Africans, confronted all too often with common White attitudes of racial pride, there was little if anything to distinguish a missionary from a colonial administrator, and most missionaries co-operated with the colonial regimes. Yet one of the most remarkable features of the modern missionary movement was its relative independence from the European colonial powers.

THE INDEPENDENCE OF MODERN MISSIONARIES

The early European missionaries in Africa, as in Asia or Latin America, had been intimately dependent on the support of secular rulers. This was most notably the case with the *padroado* agreements, by which the Portuguese crown had secured a monopolistic control over the appointment of Roman Catholic bishops, clergy and missionaries in Africa and the East Indies. These rights of patronage were one of the main factors which in part frustrated the attempts of Propaganda Fide to intervene directly by sending missionaries to Africa, and in the eighteenth century the French monarchy succeeded in establishing a similar control over priests sent to Senegal.[17] Most early Protestant missions were also strictly limited in purpose, and primarily they ministered to Europeans settled in colonies overseas. The first English society, the Society for the Propagation of the Gospel (hereafter SPG) founded in 1701, sought to assist "our loving subjects" in foreign parts who, in the words of the Society's charter, were in danger of falling into "atheism, infidelity, popish superstition and idolatry", while the Danes and the Dutch sent chaplains to their forts in West Africa and the settlement at the Cape. There were a few brief interruptions to this pattern of dependence on the state. The Capuchins in Kongo and the Moravian Brethren in South Africa had few connections with colonial powers, but overwhelmingly the early Christian missions in Africa, both Catholic and Protestant, were merely the religious arms of an increasingly secular intrusion, a decadent echo of the medieval union between church and state.

In the case of the Catholics this system was destroyed in a series of attacks inspired by rationalist criticism of Catholic philosophy and privilege. The expulsion of the Jesuits in 1759 by Pombal, the Portuguese dictator, and their subsequent dissolution deprived the mission fields of one of the most active societies. Soon after, the fury of anti-clericalism unleashed by the French Revolution and utilized by Napo-

leon, with its suppression of religious orders and confiscation
of church property, shook Catholic Europe to its foundations. This crisis, in some ways far deeper than that of the
Reformation, naturally affected the missions. For a generation there was literally no recruitment. A few priests sur-
vived for a while, but by 1820 Catholic missions in Africa
reached their lowest point since the fifteenth century. In
1834, in a late outburst of the anti-clerical, revolutionary
spirit, all religious orders were abolished in Portugal, and by
1852, when a bishop was eventually reappointed to the
vacant see of Luanda, there were only ten priests in the whole
of Angola and Mozambique, the insignificant remnants of
the *padroado*.[18] In France the early missionary societies were
suppressed by Napoleon in 1809, the year after he had entered Rome, exiled the pope and forcibly dissolved Propaganda Fide. It was only later, when the papacy began the
slow process of reconstruction, that this series of disasters
was seen in fact to have cleared the way for a completely
fresh missionary impulse, responsive to Rome's direction
and dependent no longer on the secular powers.

PROTESTANT AWAKENING

The origins of the modern Protestant missionary movement were completely different. It too had its roots in an
eighteenth-century ideological change, but John Wesley's
challenge to the established Anglican Church led not to
anti-clerical attacks, but to evangelicalism, which demanded
a renewed zeal and commitment on the part of the individual
Christian, and a deep concern for a personal act of conversion. As with German pietism which had produced the
Moravian missions, Wesley's emphasis greatly strengthened
the deepest motives for missionary work, creating an impel-
ling sense of gratitude for the gift of the Gospel and a desire
to extend its influence. But before the evangelical movement
in England was able to arouse a new interest in Protestant
missions, it had to overcome a formidable degree of hostility
and apathy. In 1786 when William Carey, an obscure Baptist
cobbler, proposed that his local meeting should form a

missionary society, the chairman replied: "Sit down, young man, when it pleases God to convert the Heathen, He'll do it without your help or mine".[19] Six years later, however, in 1792, the Baptist Missionary Society was formed; Carey sailed as its first missionary, and in a rapid chain-reaction, one group of Christians influencing the next, a series of important societies was founded. In 1795 the next link, the London Missionary Society (hereafter LMS), was forged. Aiming to be non-denominational it was in practice largely Congregational, but it in turn stimulated other Christians, notably evangelical Anglicans (Church Missionary Society, 1799), Wesleyan Methodists, and Scottish Presbyterians. The movement spread to the European mainland, with societies in the Netherlands, at Basle, in Berlin, north Germany and Paris, and it crossed the Atlantic with the American Board of Commissioners for Foreign Missions (1810) and the American Baptist Missionary Board (1814). From the 1830s onwards, the Oxford Movement brought a notable stimulus to the work of the SPG, the Universities' Mission to Central Africa (hereafter UMCA), founded in 1859, and other Anglican missions, and by the mid-century all the leading Protestant denominations were participating actively in missionary work.

By itself this chain-reaction introduced into the organization of the missionary movement a completely new element of independent strength and unity. For although at first sight the number of denominational societies seems absolutely opposed to the growth of Christian unity, the motives which inspired their formation cut right across denominational barriers. Most obviously this was the case with the evangelical societies. Recruits from Basle and the Netherlands eagerly served on CMS and LMS missions, and Sir Thomas Fowell Buxton, a Vice-President of the CMS, took the chair at an annual meeting of the Wesleyan Methodist Missionary Society, corresponded with missionaries of all denominations, and closely so-operated with John Philip of the LMS in South Africa. But co-operation and cross-fertilization were even wider than this. William Carey and Thomas Scott, the first Secretary of the CMS, deeply influenced Newman before he launched the Oxford Movement, and the High Anglican UMCA arose in response to an appeal from an LMS missionary, while the British and Foreign Bible Society, founded by evangelicals, in fact served all societies. The denominational divisions and rivalries of Christian Europe continued to hinder and mar the work in Africa, and Carey's proposal in 1810 for "a meeting of all denominations of Christians at the Cape of Good Hope" was only carried out exactly one hundred years later at Edinburgh; yet from the start the modern Protestant missionary movement exhibited an awareness of the importance and possibilities of ecumenical action, and the leaders of the societies formed on occasions a united, distinct and effective pressure group, capable both of defending missionary interests and of influencing positively European policies in Africa. In a few instances, as in the outstanding case of King Leopold's Congo Independent State, missions could challenge and help to defeat a colonial power.[20]

This new-found strength rested as well on other firm foundations. Compared with the earlier missions who often depended on state assistance and subsidies, the new societies drew their finances from a wide network of local associations. In the case of the CMS these were organized on a parish basis where possible, and the contributions came from penny collections rather than large legacies or gifts; by the 1840s the local associations were providing about £75,000 per year, some 80 per cent of the Society's income.[21] The new missions, then, depended not on the governing elite, on the establishment, but on the literate, earnest, prospering middle classes and skilled artisans, a public who made missionary periodicals the most widely circulated literature of the Victorian era. To this financial independence and wide-based support was added autonomous control: the new societies governed themselves, selected and trained their own recruits, and decided which fields to open and which policies to support. Often British and French societies still tended to choose areas where the commercial or political interests of their own nation predominated, but they had decisively broken with the earlier system where the missions had been regarded as an adjunct of the state.

CATHOLIC REVIVAL

Similar factors influenced the revival of Catholic missions, and here again the nature and organization of the new movement amounted to a revolutionary break with the past. Widespread support was mobilized with fresh sources of finance, new societies and more recruits, and at long last the papacy established an effective central direction over Catholic missions, independent of secular control. In many ways the most remarkable of the new organizations was the Association for the Propagation of the Faith, an immense fund-raising scheme, which developed from the initiative of a young Frenchwoman in the town of Lyons, who in 1819 began organizing small groups of ten persons committed to contributing a coin a week to the missions. Within three years an association based on this idea was founded in Paris. It spread rapidly, and by 1846 it was collecting over 3.5 million francs (i.e. over £140,000) per year from about 400 dioceses in Europe and America.[22] The association's role was limited to fund-raising; it itself sent no missionaries overseas, but it provided vital support at a time when the traditional financial resources of the papacy were seriously disrupted. By including influential laymen on its national committees and by appealing, like the new Protestant societies, to the artisan and middle-class laity, it tapped new sources of independent wealth to take the place of royal subsidies and feudal revenues. In particular it greatly helped the work of the new Catholic missionary societies, such as the Holy Ghost Fathers and the Society of African Missions, and in 1878 it supported Cardinal Lavigerie when he launched the White Fathers into the interior of equatorial Africa.

Rome itself took time to recover from the Napoleonic upheaval; in 1817 Propaganda Fide was re-established, but it was only under Cardinal Cappellari, who was appointed Prefect of Propaganda in 1826 and later, in 1831, became Pope as Gregory XVI until his death in 1846, that the papacy began to play a crucial role in the reorganization of the missions. Some indication of this intervention can be seen in Gregory's creation of more than seventy new ecclesiastical divisions in the mission areas. Previously vast territories were ruled by a Portuguese bishop often absent or even unappointed; now these powers were rapidly broken up and assigned to representatives of the vigorous new societies. Thus the Vicariate of the Two Guineas (1842) and that of Central Africa (1846) became the spheres of the Holy Ghost Fathers and the Verona Fathers respectively. These new divisions were ruled by a vicar apostolic chosen from the missionary societies, but dependent on Propaganda and enjoying most of the ecclesiastical powers of a bishop.

It would, however, be quite false to imagine that this reconstruction led to a vast, monolithic organization, effortlessly and entirely controlled from the centre. The true nature of Rome's influence on the missions was far more subtle, tenuous and complex, and it can best be seen in the relationship which developed between Propaganda and the new associations and societies. On the one hand, Propaganda actively assisted the expansion of the work of the Association for the Propagation of the Faith: papal privileges were given to its members, bishops were asked to support it, and in 1840 Gregory XVI himself drafted a papal encyclical, or official letter, on its behalf. In return, however, Propaganda wanted to decide how the money was spent, and it was particularly anxious lest the Association, with its headquarters in Paris, should unduly favour the work of French missions and even indirectly the imperial interests of France. In 1842 the Prefect of Propaganda suggested "an amicable participation" by which Rome could make recommendations in advance. When the Association turned down this suggestion, Propaganda responded by giving discreet support to rival fundraising organizations, and the tension between Propaganda and the Association was only finally resolved in 1922 when the Association was reorganized and its headquarters moved to Rome.[23] This disagreement undoubtedly acted as a brake to central control, but it was merely an internal tension, radically different and far less harmful to the missions than the earlier conflict over secular rights of patronage.

Turning from money to men, from the Association to, for example, the Holy Ghost Fathers, one again finds Propaganda at the centre of a delicate balance of power. Here Propaganda was able in the 1840s to insist that the old sem-

inary of the Congregation of the Holy Ghost, established by
the French monarchy to train priests for the colonies, should
be merged with a new missionary society founded by Father
Libermann, and so the French government's rights of controlling colonial priests passed effectively to Propaganda.
Sometimes owing their existence to Propaganda's support,
there were soon over fifty new Catholic missionary societies,
with recruiting houses scattered throughout Europe and
North America. Generally they were far more responsive
to Propaganda's control than the older orders with their
entrenched traditional allegiances and territorial interests.
Thus it is no coincidence that they were the favoured instruments for Rome's intervention in Africa, and in the twentieth
century there were about forty Catholic societies at work
there.

FREEDOM FROM SECULAR CONTROL

The most obvious consequence, then, for Africa, of the new
missionary movements, both Protestant and Catholic, was
their capacity to harness a widespread, continuous, sacrificial
response, which maintained an increasing momentum of
evangelization even while Africa's climate remained uncon-
quered. In West and equatorial Africa large numbers of
missionaries continued to be killed by disease for most of the
nineteenth century, but the reinforcements and fresh initiatives were far greater than before. Increasingly, again in
striking contrast to earlier centuries, these reinforcements
included women, either in religious orders, or single, or as
the wives of missionaries, and a new dimension was therefore opened as the Gospel was carried direct to African
women.

The nineteenth-century revolution in missionary work in
Africa was, however, by no means limited merely to this
vast new influx of missionaries, assisted by the technological
and other changes of the industrial revolution. With their
broad network of contributors and recruits, with their
journals mobilizing the newly literate public, and with their
systems of autonomous control, the new bases decisively

liberated the work of evangelization from the shackles of secular control. For Catholic missions the fruits of this independence were mainly ecclesiastical: they could now operate far beyond colonial or commercial frontiers, and later, during the colonial period, Rome proved able to continue and expand her work under Catholic, anti-clerical, or Protestant governments alike. The African career of Cardinal Lavigerie, one of the most outstanding missionary strategists in the history of the church, is indeed wholly an illustration of this new freedom: whether in his early assertion in Algiers of the right to work among Muslims, or in his spectacular thrust into Equatoria and his subsequent hard-fought negotiations with King Leopold for the control of the upper Congo. To a very large extent his impact on Africa depended on his intimate links in Europe both with the papacy and Propaganda, with influential political circles, and with the media of mass support.[24]

Missionaries in colonial Africa were, of course, still deeply influenced by church–state relationships in Europe. The *Kulturkampf*, the *Loi de la Séparation*, the *Risorgimento* and the Lateran treaties all meant that Catholic missionaries from Germany, France, Belgium and Italy approached the colonial state from a profoundly different standpoint from that of Anglo-Saxon and Scandinavian missionaries. In Britain the missionary societies and their supporters were at the heart of the humanitarian movement. Under Sir Thomas Fowell Buxton this influence reached a peak with the 1841 Niger Expedition and John Philip's defence of African rights in South Africa,[25] but even after this early period the humanitarian pressure groups continued to operate, and some missionaries were attentive critics of the more obvious colonial abuses. Occasionally they produced not merely a critic but a constructive statesman like J.H. Oldham, even if, as we have been reminded, his vision was severely limited by the prevalent paternalist assumptions.[26] Untrammelled by a colonial nexus with Africa, missionaries in the United States and Scandinavia could contribute even more freely and sometimes more effectively to the maintenance of an international humanitarian tradition.[27] It may well be that the role of these missions in shaping international attitudes to Africa will emerge as being of much greater significance than their direct political influence in Africa itself.

The contrast with continental Catholicism, and France in particular, could hardly be greater. Numerically, the French contribution to African missions in the latter nineteenth and early twentieth centuries was immense. In North Africa, Lavigerie, and in equatorial Africa, Augouard notably assisted the expansion of French colonial rule, but the divide between church and state in the Third Republic would seem to have inhibited any intimate missionary influence on official colonial policy. It appears to have prohibited even the existence of an humanitarian lobby which could mobilize both free-thinkers and ecclesiastics. The debate on philosophical principles precluded any effective discussion of practical morality. Reluctantly the state tolerated the continued existence of the missionary orders, and for the missionaries the state in the colonies as in the metropole remained primarily an antagonist, a rival against which one had continually to be on guard, wresting from it whatever slender advantages one could as a meagre return for services rendered, or so at least it would seem to an outside observer with no specialist knowledge against which to check this impression. Perhaps it is indicative of the inattention paid to the missionary factor in France that the only entries under "missionaries" in the index of Henri Brunschwig's *French Colonialism 1871–1941* (English translation, London, 1964) refer to British Protestant missionaries. Certainly there would seem to be room for a thorough assessment of the relationship between missions and state in France and in the French empire, and an examination of Augouard's career might well provide an admirable starting point.[28]

The consequences for independent Africa of these very different missionary attitudes to the colonial state have yet to be fully investigated. The legacy is perhaps most evident in the case of Zaïre. As in France, church–state relations, particularly over the control of education, dominated Belgian politics in the early twentieth century, but in Belgium the Catholic Party was far more powerful and it continued to participate in every government throughout the inter-war period, being particularly influential in the ministry of colonies.[29] In the Congo, therefore, the colonial state was seen by Belgian missionaries not merely as a source of financial assistance for educational and other work but also as an ally against the forces of European anti-clericalism: a dimension of political ideology was here introduced which was absent in the more pragmatic arrangements entered into elsewhere between missions and colonial governments. As with the French, the preoccupations and divisions of the European scene had been exported to Africa, but in this case with diametrically opposite results. It is therefore hardly surprising that resentment against this alliance formed an important strand in the nationalist protest of black *evolués*, nor that Zaïre has witnessed the most dramatic conflict, at least in the classic terms of institutional leadership, between church and state in independent Africa. Yet, though much of the polemic of both sides has continued to make use of the formulas fashioned earlier in Europe,[30] the actual course of the dispute, the alternation of challenge and reconciliation, has demonstrated, particularly since the Africanization of the episcopate, a peculiarly African rhythm rather than a pattern suggested by European logic.[31]

MISSIONS AND COMMUNICATIONS

For Africa as a whole, however, the consequences of the relative independence of the modern missionary movement were in no sphere more significant than in the revolutionary changes that were taking place in the techniques of communication in sub-Saharan Africa. Independent of the state, missions, albeit for their own interests, could introduce innovations of critical important for Africans. For the third and final point to be mentioned in refuting the thesis that the recent rapid growth of Christianity in Black Africa was directly dependent on the establishment and extension of European colonial rule, is that such a proposition grossly exaggerates the significance of the colonial interlude in African history. As has been remarked elsewhere, there have been two great watersheds in the history of Africa during the last seven millenia, changes that have profoundly altered the whole social environment of most of the continent. The first was the transition to food production; the second was the modern revolution in the means of communication. This transformation "began, not with colonial rule, but with the steamers, railways, telegraph, vernacular bibles, and newspapers of the nineteenth century"[32] and Christian missions were often able to play a decisive role in pioneering these momentous changes. Their early commitment to the alliance between "Christianity and commerce", to eradicate the slave trade and to bring the interior into direct contact with the Christian world, led them to become the foremost innovators. It was the missions and their humanitarian allies, who campaigned for the opening up of the Niger; it was the missions, following in David Livingstone's footsteps, who placed their steamers on the navigable Congo and on Lakes Malawi and Tanganyika. But their material contribution was by no means limited to these major, well-known facts. Virtually every mission station brought with it examples of technological change. In some cases it was that ancient invention, the wheel, that they introduced. Thus the Verona missionaries, re-establishing the Catholic initiative in the southern Sudan in the early twentieth century, were horrified at the system of forced human porterage that radiated out from the riverhead at Wau. Instead they constructed oxcarts, and rejoiced in liberating man "from the shame of being used as a beast of burden".[33]

LITERACY

But the missions' link with more modern means of transport was incidental to their main purpose. Nor was it their most important contribution to communications in Africa. Far more central and crucial was the role of Christianity as a proponent of literacy. All Protestant missionaries shared the aim of bringing the Bible to Africa. Because of their deep desire that African Christians should be able "to search the Scriptures", many Protestant missions even insisted that the acquisition of literacy was a prerequisite for baptism. While rejecting this stipulation as an unwarranted obstacle to membership of a Christian community, African Christian prophets equally proclaimed and manifested their reverence for God's word. It was with Bible in hand that the Prophet Harris cast out evil, and the distinguishing mark of most African Christian prophets has been that they are men or women of the Bible. Catholic missions laid rather less emphasis on literacy. The catechism, rather than the Bible, was often for them the first priority, and in some missions in the early days, as with the White Fathers among the Bemba,[34] the catechism was mainly learnt by rote, in much the same way as Muslim teaching had been communicated for centuries in the Qur'ānic schools of Black Africa.

Yet, whereas in sub-Saharan African Islam literacy had been restricted effectively to a relatively small number of learned Muslims, even Catholic missions powerfully contributed to the spread of literacy. Books of devotions, lives of the saints, and selections from the scriptures, as well as catechisms, were all translated fairly rapidly by Catholics. The Christian propagation of literacy involved a massive penetration into African languages. Unlike the Qur'ān and the main Islamic works of learning, which had remained tightly anchored to the Arabic original, Christian teaching and literature became rapidly accessible in many African vernaculars.[35] Pioneer missionaries quickly recognized the strategic significance of literacy. As an American missionary remarked: "Ours is the opportunity to provide the only literature they will have for many years to come. Would it not thrill you to think that you controlled the reading matter of an entire tribe?"[36] Such arrogantly paternal sentiments might well exaggerate the power that the production of this literature bestowed on missionaries, for the mission could not control the individual's interpretation of the Bible and Christian teaching, but his remarks underline the revolution in communications that their activity was initiating.

In order to introduce and exploit this new technique, all Christian missions found themselves in some degree committed to establishing schools. Their commitment varied from the rather reluctant provision of the most elementary classes, to the enthusiastic planning by Robert Laws in Malawi of courses he hoped would lead to a university curriculum.[37] Yet, whatever the attitude of different missions toward education, whether they viewed it as a diversion from their evangelistic aims or an integral means of creating a new Christian community, African demand for education soon ensured that the provision and maintenance of schools rapidly became the distinctive activity of Christian missions in Africa.[38] And because the missions could mobilize funds and teachers independently of state support, they were able in many cases to provide this crucial service to Africa long before the colonial regimes sought to control this process. When at last colonial rulers awoke to the incipient dangers and challenge to their authority posed by what one of them, the governor-general of Nigeria, termed this "extraordinary irruption of hedge-schools",[39] the African renaissance had already begun. The colonial powers could not turn back the clock; missionary education had become the Achilles' heel of colonialism.

COMMUNICATIONS AND COSMOLOGY

Christianity had thus powerfully contributed to the radical transformation of communications in sub-Saharan Africa. Its participation in this revolutionary process was not, however, limited to the mere provision of new techniques, be they steamers or mass literacy. It was intimately involved with these changes at a deeper, cosmological basis. And it is perhaps at this level that one can perceive the most striking contrast with Islam. Much earlier, Muslims had developed the vital trans-Saharan communications, and had subsequently been responsible for bringing Black Africa into closer contact with the civilizations of North Africa and the Middle East. Islam had thus been concerned with the social and political changes associated with long-distance trade, but this commerce had been limited in its economic impact. Muslims had not introduced a new technology. In tropical Africa, with its parasitic diseases, modernization and the communications revolution had to await the arrival of steampower, the internal-combustion engine, and electronics. The new technology, which at first sight bestowed on its Western possessors something of the status of gods, had been the consequence in Europe of a cosmological revolution, a profound and radical change in the way men regarded nature and the universe. In its origins this scientific revolution, which lay behind the inventions and new technology, had owed something to early Islamic and Ancient Greek thought, but essentially it had developed in Christendom. Early Western science had been built on the Christian belief in the potential and freedom of man within God's creation, and, in its turn, Christianity, alone of the world religions, had been forced, albeit gradually and hesitantly, to come to terms with the claims and assumptions of the scientists. The results can clearly be seen in the changing world view of Christian missionaries in Africa. Whereas in the sixteenth and seventeenth centuries European missionaries, in accord with African cosmologies, believed that spiritual forces were responsible for most of the events determining the course of human life, by the nineteenth and twentieth centuries this wide range of causation had been considerably curtailed. Modern missionaries therefore generally had little patience with fears of witchcraft, and they relied on pills almost as much as on prayer for a defence against illness. Simultaneously, missionaries claimed that the secrets and wonder of the new inventions could rightly be understood only in the light of the freedom and order inherent in the Christian revelation. Or, to put it in popular parlance, the Bible had made Europe powerful. Many Westerners, missionaries included, forgetting the universal implications of this insight, went on to assume that their technological superiority was inherently linked, not with science, but with Caucasian ethnic origins, so that for them Christianity became part of a White man's package of "civilization" to be thrust on Africans with varying degrees of force. But despite these absurd aberrations, the fact remained that for most Africans, confronted with the turmoil of modernization initiated and intensified by the communications revolution, Christianity alone presented a set of beliefs and ideas which, at one end of the spectrum embraced their traditional spiritual needs and concerns, and at the other enabled them to reach out and comprehend some of the new forces that were so radically altering their whole environment.

CHAPTER 5

Christianity and Concepts of Evil in Sub-Saharan Africa

A central problem for Christianity in twentieth-century Africa has been whether two very different concepts of evil can interact and, in doing so, provide a momentum for social and political change. For Christians in sub-Saharan Africa have set out to define evil from two widely separated starting points. The first perspective owed much to Western Christianity and has a relatively clear focus: in many respects it has developed from those strands in Christianity which have sought to apply biblical ethical insights to social, economic and political challenges. The second perspective took as its starting point ancient and deeply established African concepts, and it appealed to African traditions of summoning spiritual resources to defend the individual and the community against the consequences of evil.

The first perspective was forcefully represented by those independent Black Christians whom Sundkler characterized as Ethiopians.[1] The distinctive evils which were challenged by their Christian faith were racial discrimination and white domination in church and state. These facets of colonialism were measured against biblical teaching and were clearly revealed as manifestations of evil. The Ethiopians, like other Christians in Africa, did not hesitate to invoke the biblical symbol of Satan, which carries, as we shall see, far-reaching implications. This vision was forcefully expressed by Charles Domingo, the former servant and protégé of Robert Laws of Livingstonia. Some time between 1907 and 1910 Domingo broke with the Presbyterian mission, formed his own church and went on to proclaim: "The gainers of Money and Missionaries are very poor to try to conquer the wiles of Satan ... [They] do form the same rule to look upon the native with mockery eyes".[2] Domingo, Elliott Kamwana and John Chilembwe exercised this prophetic ministry in Nyasaland, suffered, were imprisoned and even died for it.

In a sense these Ethiopians stood squarely within a great tradition of Christian missionary humanitarian concern. In Africa this stretched back to abolition and beyond it to the protests in the sixteenth and seventeenth centuries when missionaries and Black Christians had asserted the principle of basic human rights against the iniquities of the slave trade.[3] It is therefore by no means surprising to find that the Ethiopians' challenge to racial discrimination was shared by many African Christians within the missionary-connected churches, especially those which fostered an articulate political education, as did Robert Laws. Before World War I, while Domingo was breaking with the Presbyterians, other members of this church were forming welfare associations with missionary encouragement. Donald Siwale, one of the pioneer members of these embryonic political organizations, later recalled that "our idea of equality came from the Bible"[4] and in 1947 the young Kenneth Kaunda spoke to a Scots missionary at Lubwa of racial oppression as a "great burden of evil".[5] This implication of the Gospel was also clearly grasped and expressed even among those denominations which were least open to liberal insights. Justo Mwale, the first African minister of the South African-based Dutch Reformed Mission in Zambia, became a leader of *Msonkhano wokweza dziko* ("meeting to develop the country") which was linked by Gerdien Verstraelen's informants with the "beginnings of politics".[6] At these meetings the colour bar was criticized, and another colleague of Justo Mwale is remembered as "very independent, always strong in preaching and emphasising that black and white are the same".[7]

Christians did not merely denounce racial injustice. Gradually Christians in Africa have been led into a deeper analysis of their situation, an analysis focused on alienation and exploitation. At the great Jerusalem meeting of the International Missionary Council in 1928, R.H. Tawney, when discussing the growth of industrialization in the mission territories, enunciated "the claim of religion to control, not a part, but the whole of human life".[8] As the Copperbelt developed, the implications of this claim were set out by Godfrey Wilson and Mike Moore, who challenged the exploitative system of migrant labour, disrupted families and disastrously inadequate wages.[9] Later, as the struggle for liberation intensified in Southern Africa, Albert Nolan, one of the founders of the Institute of Contextual Theology in Braamfontein, insisted that

> Searching for the signs of the times in the spirit of Jesus . . . will mean recognising all the forces that are working against man as the forces of evil. Is the present world order not ruled and governed by Satan, the enemy of man? Is the system not the modern equivalent of the kingdom of Satan? . . . To believe in Jesus is to believe that goodness can and will triumph over evil. Despite the system . . . man can be, and in the end will be, liberated.[10]

Yet had the appeal of Christianity in Africa been limited to the denunciation of racial discrimination or even the exploitation which often accompanied the extension of capitalist enterprises, it might well have remained primarily the concern of a small educated elite or socially conscious minority. Many Africans, however, when first confronted with the Gospel, have appropriated Christianity as a powerful new reinforcement in the conflict with a radically differing concept of evil. This second perspective begins by instinctively sensing as evil all that detracts from or destroys life. Illness, infertility, pestilence, famine and sudden or inexplicable death are the manifestations of evil, and these experiences are seldom if ever the result of mere chance or misfortune. This concept has an explanatory function. Beliefs in taboo and witchcraft help in some measure to make intelligible, and therefore bearable, the recurrent threats of hunger, disease and a fearful incidence of infant mortality. Just as the doctrine of Providence can reduce for believers in the Jewish, Christian and Muslim traditions the despair and anguish of blind fate or chance, so these theories of evil in Africa can bring an element of courage, comfort and calm resignation. But this explanatory function is also intimately connected with ethics. The intervention of the hostile powers of evil can be provoked either by one's own behaviour when taboos are broken, or by the wishes and actions of sorcerers or witches. In both cases, ethical values are involved. Selfishness, the neglect of the rights of other people whether living or dead, adultery, the destruction of categories,[11] all these could provoke punishment by ancestral and other spiritual powers. "The wages of sin is death", and the sin need not have been one's own. The envy, hatred and jealousy of others, whether justified or not, could activate malignant mystical forces against one. In terrible, exceptional cases, malice could become personified, take possession of someone, ultimately change his or her personality, and direct its destruction indiscriminately, and sometimes even unconsciously, upon the community. Thus in Africa, as in many other parts of the world, the whole range of different meanings which in English have been translated by the word "evil" – running from the purely descriptive "bad" through "immoral" or "wicked" to "radically evil"[12] – often remain closely interconnected.

Partly because misfortune and suffering were so closely linked in many African societies with ethical transgressions, the missionaries' denunciations of sin struck a strong responsive chord, even if most Africans did not immediately comprehend the missionaries' sense of sin as evil interiorized, involving individual responsibility and personal guilt. After having the ten commandments explained to him, one Yao chief told a Yao Anglican priest "if these are the words you have brought us, we welcome them, for none like stealing, murdering, adultery or lying, though we commit them", and another Yao chief "hailed as a grand and certain result of Christianity spreading in his country, the fact that witchcraft will be driven out before it".[13] Christianity was indeed sometimes seen as but the latest in a series of purification or witchcraft-eradication movements.[14] As migrant workers returned to their villages bearing with them their understandings of the Gospel, their testimonies were often greeted as the proclamation of yet another source of spiritual power which brought assistance in age-old conflicts with evil.[15]

This reaction and resonance was enormously enhanced as Africans began to read the biblical healing narratives. Suddenly they discovered that most Western missionaries in the nineteenth century had overlooked in their presentation of the kerygma a theme to which the writers of both the Old and New Testaments had given much prominence. It was a theme of immense relevance to Africa. It carried a deep congruence with the religious concerns of most Africans; and then, as Africans increasingly found themselves marginalized by mercantile and industrial capitalism, biblical healing began to provide them with a resource with which to resist the hardships and anomie of proletarianization.[16] In the first quarter of the twentieth century, the great prophetic leaders, Harris and Braide in coastal West Africa, Kimbangu and Shembe in Central and Southern Africa, mightily proclaimed its relevance. And this discovery was by no means restricted to independent Africans. It was of course a major, distinctive emphasis of Pentecostalist missionaries. One suspects also that an emphasis on Christian spiritual healing has been far more widespread within the mainline, mission-connected churches than has previously been recognized. Elsewhere attention has been drawn to those elements in African Catholicism which have emphasized miraculous interventions in the lives of individuals and communities. There was much in missionary Catholicism which elicited a ready response in Africa: the lavish use of holy water to purify and exorcize, to cure disease and to protect homes and crops; the wearing of rosaries and Marian medals as distinctive, protective symbols; the cults of the saints, especially that of St Thérèse of Lisieux with reports of her widespread miracles of healing. All these were brought by the missionaries. To them, the catechist added some of the functions of traditional diviners and ritual experts as he was called on to solve local disputes, lead prayers for the sick and for those gripped by the fear of evil powers, prepare the troubled for Confession and baptize the dying.[17] And, as more is discovered concerning the spirituality of local Christian communities in Africa, these instances may prove to be but the tip of the iceberg.

One way of interpreting this appropriation of Christianity by popular prophetic movements is to claim that the new religion becomes part of basic unchanged African cosmologies.[18] I would argue that a far more fruitful approach is found in Lamin Sanneh's insistence that the African response

E

to Christianity derives its force and vitality from indigenous models and experiences. But this is very different from asserting that African religious concepts have remained unchanged by Christianity. Africans' tolerance of religious diversity and their inclusive view of community have contrasted sharply with Western ethnocentric (or Semitic?) exclusivism and have provided a milieu for deep and vigorous interactions.[19] On its side, the Bible (and of course the Qur'ān) has introduced into Africa a store a potent symbols. They provide a focus for an expanding array of different meanings. They evoke therefore a response which, initially at least, meets a variety of needs. Their creative freedom helps to establish what Weber termed "the idiosyncratic autonomy of the religious domain".[20] This encounter between symbolic messages, this process of mutual enrichment, can be sudden. It can produce a burst of enthusiasm, sweeping hundreds or even thousands into a religious movement, as in the response to Harris or Kimbangu. When part of a literate and universal tradition, however, the process can be long-term and cumulative. The influence of a scriptural symbol can be exerted contemporaneously in many varied situations or chronologically over very different periods.[21]

Among the biblical symbols is Satan as a personification of evil. Around this symbol can be gathered diverse understandings of evil, which enable it to exert a powerful, dominant influence. The symbol of Satan also brings with it other referents linked to sacraments and scriptures, for a contrasting referent to Satan in the New Testament is the Kingdom of God.[22] We must therefore examine the ways in which these symbols have altered African concepts of evil, and in particular the ways in which they have enabled the two different perspectives of evil to meet and to enrich each other. Steven Kaplan has pointed out that Satan has been "the forgotten 'man' of Ethiopian history as written by modern scholars". Kaplan argues persuasively that in medieval Ethiopia the idiom of Satanic activities served to pinpoint social and political tensions. The monastic saints of Ethiopia armed with their "arsenal of holy water, the cross, prayers and power derived from God, did battle with and defeated the forces which threatened to disrupt society".[23]

The time-scale of Christianity in Ethiopia is more akin to that of Islam in the Sudanic belt, but something of the same process can be seen in studies of more recent developments. In his analysis of Christianity and politics in a small area of Kenya, Sangree has described how the concept of Satan and his works has supplied for the Tiriki "a conceptualization and personification of *all evil*, whereas before beliefs about witches served as a looser, rather less inclusive focus for beliefs about evil".[24] That is a most fruitful insight. It suggests something of the potential of this symbol, and of the dynamism which can gather around it. Only too easily, this dynamism can become a frightening and terrible instrument, as the witch-hunts in Europe and North America demonstrated. But the potential can also develop in positive directions. As we shall see, in their challenge to the fears associated with witchcraft, Christian communities have gradually moved from a concern to identify witches to a trust in the protection offered by baptism, prayer and worship. And the defeat of Satan in any of his guises, release from the power of evil wherever it is encountered, involves yet another metaphor: the coming of the Kingdom.

The introduction, almost imperceptible at times, of this second, profoundly evangelic proclamation is encountered even at humble healing sessions which draw equally on Christian and traditional symbolism and cosmologies. A completely uneducated patient, attending a healing service of the prophet Luamba in the lower Zaïre as described by Janzen, would, after hymn-singing and biblical teaching, be anointed with oil while the prophet intoned the following prayer or some variation of it:

> Father! You have wisdom
> Sufficient to heal
>   All sufferings,
>   All illnesses.
> I do not possess herbs and medicines,
> But that which I have I give you.
> (*Laying hands on the patient*)
> In the name of Jesus,
> Release the fount of health,

Release it upon his thoughts,
Release it upon his whole being.
Give him peace.
Open the fount of blessing.
Open it upon you!
In Jesus' name I say:
    Suffering!
    All sicknesses!
    Be still!
    Be still in Jesus' name!
Again I say:
    All suffering!
    And all sicknesses!
    Release this person!
    Release God's person!
The possessor of this mind,
And these, your thoughts,
And your body and strength.
Father, may the hand of God heal,
And there where the pain is,
May it vanish.
If the health is choked out,
By the hands of evil ones,
May they release it!
May you regain health at work!
Oh, Blessed Father,
Father of peace.
May your name be honoured,
May your kingdom come.[25]

The purification ritual employed by Luamba is in origin pre-Christian, but must one conclude from this that the cosmology has remained unaltered? From Janzen's account it would seem that Christian elements and symbols are becoming increasingly prominent in this and similar movements. A sufferer who previously found healing in a totally pre-Christian cult of affliction now finds him or herself confronted with Christian concepts in a context which yet remains readily comprehensible to the patient in terms of a traditional cosmology. Subsequently the patient might well encounter the same Christian concepts and symbols in a different environment and applied to problems remote from such a cosmology. Reconciliation, justice and peace can assume other, larger dimensions. The Kingdom of Heaven can take on new implications. Evil can be revealed as many-faceted. The works of Satan are perceived not only in individual human malice, but also in corporate greed and structural exploitation. In a religion which seeks to embrace the whole world, a ritual symbol, instead of being tied to a specific, particular situation, can begin to acquire a universal significance.

Of all the movements which drew inspiration from the Bible, the Watchtower adherents, a central African development from the Jehovah's Witnesses, laid the most dramatic emphasis on the figure of Satan and on Satanic influences in the world. Watchtower's initial impact in Africa challenged not merely colonial abuses but the ideological structure of colonial rule. All governments were regarded as Satanic, and the organized churches were seen as Satan's emissaries. Karen Fields has persuasively argued that in the 1920s Watchtower provided Central Africans with a consistent, intelligible ideology.[26] With its help they could respond positively to the appalling circumstances in which colonial pressures had placed them. Far from being merely a confused, hysterical symptom of stress and anomie, in which images of biblical apocalyptic were jumbled together with African beliefs, Watchtower represented a coherent, readily understood challenge to colonial rule. For the colonial state, like the medieval one, exploited the organizational and ideological resources of religion. Colonial administrators relied on the co-operation of customary rulers, whose authority was often derived from their religious sanctions. Christian missionaries were also used as sources of intelligence and social control. Africans were therefore at least partly correct when they asserted that the forces arrayed against them were religious in character.

Many Africans readily perceived their sufferings in a religious idiom. The trauma of World War I, the pressures of taxation and labour recruitment, and the demands of missionaries which threatened the basic identity of many

Africans were all most easily understood by equating them with witchcraft, with the form of evil most familiar to them.[27] Watchtower baptism was often seen as providing a defence against witchcraft. In Lomagundi in Southern Rhodesia this emphasis was explicit. Baptism "was thought of as making it impossible for the 'dipped' person ever again to bewitch or to be bewitched".[28] In Northern Rhodesia, people who refused such baptism were accused of witchcraft and were called "*wasatani*, or devils".[29] In this way, Watchtower baptism challenged the customary powers of the chiefs, and so threatened the basic relationship of the colonial order. Around this potent symbol of evil, Watchtower mobilized mass protests against a whole range of grievances. Its baptism was an effective political weapon because it exposed the fragility of colonial rule. Officials suddenly glimpsed the potential of "People's Power". Watchtower leaders may have been mistaken in predicting that colonial rule would so soon give way to the millennium; but, Fields argues, "when people finally ask themselves How Long? and answer back, Not long! they are already in motion".[30]

At times this apocalyptic vision led Africans to articulate explicit political and social demands, which echoed the convictions of Siwale, Kaunda and the whole tradition of political education associated with the Scottish missionaries of Livingstonia. A group of Watchtower adherents arrested at a mine in the Katanga in August 1936 stated

> It stands out clearly from this book [The Bible] that all men are equal. God did not create the white man to rule over the black. . . . It is not just that the black man who does the work should remain in poverty and misery, and that the wages of the whites should be so much higher than those of the blacks.[31]

Watchtower embodied then a protest which alarmed colonial governments, and in 1938 the Pan-Africanist C.L.R. James hailed Watchtower as "the most powerful revolutionary force in Africa today".[32] An emphasis on healing traditional evils was, however, present also from the start, and gradually Watchtower's political protest and challenge to colonial rule seem to have faded. In 1950 an anthropologist observing an assembly of Jehovah's Witnesses in the Luapula area thought that the appeal of their teaching as an antidote to witchcraft was one of its major features; but, after independence, African governments have again seen their millenarian emphases as a political challenge.[33]

A somewhat similar progression from a concern with the results of evil in economic and social structures to a profound preoccupation with the supernatural background to sickness can, at first sight, be seen in the life of one of Africa's most internationally renowned Christian healers, Archbishop Emmanuel Milingo. As a young parish priest in a peri-urban area of Lusaka, Milingo was active in social work and also became a very effective broadcaster as secretary for communications for the Zambia Episcopal Conference. He became well known in Zambia through his broadcasts, and he began to champion the cause of the underprivileged. He created the Lusaka Helpers' Club which mobilized wealthier Christians to succour the inhabitants of the shanty towns. In 1969, three years after arriving in Lusaka, he was appointed its archbishop. His involvement with and concern for the poor led him to be very conscious of their problems, which they themselves saw arising from the activities of spirits. In 1973 he discovered he had been given the charisma of healing and exorcism. In the phenomenon of spirit possession, Milingo saw "a deep pastoral and missionary problem". Those who felt they were possessed "have a right to the liberating power of Jesus Christ". Those who were healed "have come to know that God cares for them. They have realised that God is powerful above all other gods. They give up their beliefs in the agents of the evil one. . . . They are redeemed and liberated from the tyranny of demonic possession"[34].

In the popular press Archbishop Milingo is identified solely with exorcism and dramatic healings, but the published record reveals a more complex approach to evil. His increasing involvement with the healing of distressed individuals did not banish his concern with other aspects of evil. Before his recall to Rome in 1982, he continued to seek to awaken the consciences of the privileged elite. At the jubilee celebrations in July 1978 he was not afraid to criticize "those who hold high offices in Government or business . . . who enjoy being considered Christians, but as a matter of fact they are not". In guarded language he also implicitly compared those politicians, who accept international loans which lay onerous obligations on the whole nation, with individuals who "make pacts with the devil".[35] But in developing his intuitive sympathy with those who are bearing the brunt of Zambia's uneven development, he increasingly spoke in terms more readily understood by the poor and uneducated. It was no coincidence that the majority of those who came to seek his help were women, for it was they who suffered most both in the rural areas and in the towns. In his account of his fight with the evil spirits, Milingo describes how the poor see "each day as a torture" which they cannot escape.[36] In identifying their adversary as Satan and in assisting them to find a Christian liberation, he may well have demonstrated a way to raise their consciousness, to restore their hope and self-respect and gradually, bearing in mind the cumulative impact of a symbol, to broaden their vision of the realities which faced them. The theological standpoints of Watchtower and a Catholic archbishop are, of course, far removed in many respects, but these examples do illustrate that the new dimensions of evil, facilitated by a common symbol, do not necessarily lead from so-called "traditional" to "modern" concerns. The emphasis may turn from politics to a more intimate concern with the individual patient. But the fact that the cosmology has been restructured, that its central feature is now the conflict between the Kingdom of God and its Satanic adversaries, has resulted in radically new concepts of the nature of evil and of how to confront it.

Perhaps the most spectacular movement of mass conversion in Africa was that which developed from the preaching of the Grebo prophet from Liberia, William Wade Harris, who, in a mission lasting less than two years, persuaded thousands of men and women in southern Ivory Coast and Gold Coast to turn towards faith in a new understanding of God's power and authority. Recent research has considerably clarified the biblical foundations and structure of Harris' thought and preaching. He was someone who had deeply appropriated the insights of the prophet Daniel and those of the Book of Revelation.[37] Research has also thrown light on how his beliefs challenged and transformed the concept of evil. Like many other Christian healers and prophets in Africa, Harris saw baptism as a means of providing the protection of an Almighty God to people wracked with the fears of sorcery and witchcraft. He commanded his converts to renounce reliance on traditional charms, "fetish" or objects of power. In itself this was no new demand. It was a common theme in many pre-Christian movements of regeneration and purification. Fetish was always an ambiguous power. When controlled and used for the whole community, it was beneficient and legitimate. But when a charm was used secretly for personal profit and advancement, it was evil. Hence a demand to turn from one set of charms to a new, public legitimate source of supernatural power was always liable to evoke an enthusiastic welcome. Yet Harris carried this demand into a new dimension. Former charms and fetish were now condemned as works of the devil. God was proclaimed as all-powerful. There was what has been termed "a theocratic reorganization" of the cosmos.[38] When practising exorcism, Harris commanded Satan to come out of individuals. He also prohibited the practice of interrogating corpses to discover whose act of witchcraft was responsible for their death. Instead he encouraged people to confess their sins and failings, for as God's prophet he also brought God's judgement. Evil was seen to stem from personal disobedience rather than from external attack, and for Harris and his converts belief in God's power began to eradicate the fear of witchcraft.

The message of the judgement of an all-powerful God carried, however, other implications. Harris proclaimed a new order, a new Jerusalem, which transcended the power of the white colonial regimes. "I am sent," he said when condemning Sunday work in the docks at Sekondi, "to preach rebellion. God is making use of me, a Kroo man, for his purpose." He condemned the colonial powers for their pursuit of "money religion" and for their involvement in the godless bloodshed of World War I. In claiming the judgeship promised in the twentieth chapter of the Book of Revelation, he was aware that he was confronting the beast – that symbol of any political power which demands absolute loyalty.

"Only God" he said, "has power over me", and when expelled from the Ivory Coast he remained convinced that God would send fire on Abidjan and Bingerville "because the French government serves the devil and not the true God".[39] Here again biblical symbols were producing in Africa new and complex insights into the nature of evil.

One of the clearest examples of the process by which individuals when joined together in a Christian community have discovered new insights into the nature and dimensions of evil is provided by Farai David Muzorewa's account of the Rukwadzano women's movement in Zimbabwe, although we have little detailed explicit information concerning their use of symbols. Founded at Old Umtali Methodist Mission in 1929 by the wives of ministers and pastor-teachers, the movement's first objective was "a burning desire" to improve husband–wife relationships. It was born in the ecstasy of revival fervour. Under its charismatic leader, Mrs Lydia Chimonyo, "prayer for the guidance of the Holy Spirit" was a central feature of the movement.

> "Members", Muzorewa reports, "constantly give testimonies to the 'miraculous' powers of healing, exorcism and conversion. . . . They believe implicitly that Jesus's words, 'Ask, and it shall be given you' (Matt. 7:7), are fulfilled as barren women ask for babies and become pregnant, evil spirits are cast out, and unfaithful husbands become once again loyal to their wives".[40]

These Methodist matrons were, and are, manifestly aware of the age-old needs of rural Africa, and the annual five-day outdoor camp meeting is the scene for "all-night informal prayer sessions seeking individual conversions, healings or exorcisms". For many of these women, the Kingdom of God initially represented release from the old evils of jealousy, fear and frustration encompassed in beliefs involving witchcraft and spirit possession. From the start, however, they have combined these prayer sessions and revival meetings with works of charity: the collection of old clothes, food and money for the sick and poverty-stricken. Increasingly the movement was established in the large urban centres of Harare and Bulawayo where wives migrated with their husbands. These experiences, the awareness that they were part of a national movement, together with travel further afield by some of their members, resulted in a heightened social and political awareness in the movement. Their concept of the Kingdom acquired new dimensions. As educational openings for Africans were restricted under the Smith regime, the women responded by building schools, providing scholarships and establishing adult education and handicraft training programmes and centres. In 1964 and 1970 they took part, after a week of prayer, in massive demonstrations against the banning of their church leaders. Above all they gained self-confidence. They acquired a new vision of the evils of racial and political oppression and of economic exploitation. Through prayer and action their understanding of the Kingdom was widened and deepened.

One of the most recent and profoundly important African examples of the implications of a Christian understanding of evil is *The Kairos Document*. Signed in 1985 by more than 150 South African theologians, Black and White, the document opens with a searching critique of "State" and "Church Theology". Unreservedly the Kairos theologians condemn the state's use of the label "communist" as its symbol of evil, and they denounce as blasphemy the appeal, in the preamble to the apartheid constitution, to Almighty God "who gathered our forebears together from many lands and gave them this their own". Here, the Kairos theologians assert

> We have a god who is historically on the side of the white settlers, who dispossesses black people of their land and who gives the major part of the land to his "chosen people".... The god of the South African State is not merely an idol or false god, it is the devil disguised as Almighty God – the antichrist.[41]

To those White church leaders who urge the need for reconciliation as an absolute Christian principle, they respond by stating that the conflict is a struggle "between justice and injustice, good and evil, God and the devil". Reconciliation and peace can be sought only when "the present injustices have been removed". The Kairos theologians end by calling for the church to clarify the contemporary significance of its own rituals:

> The evil forces we speak of in baptism must be named. We know what these evil forces are in South Africa today. The unity and sharing we profess in our communion services or Masses must be named. It is the solidarity of the people inviting all to join in the struggle for God's peace in South Africa. The repentance we preach must be named. It is repentance for our share of the guilt for the suffering and oppression in our country.[42]

This uncompromising document was welcomed with astonished joy in the Black townships. Significantly it also drew into this debate representatives of those African churches whose concerns have been focused historically on the need for healing from illnesses caused by the activities of evil spirits. Earlier, in 1984, Archbishop Ngada, one of the signatories of *The Kairos Document*, had published a fascinating account of a pilot study conducted by himself and other members of the churches of the people. This had reviewed their theological insights and had emphasized their African heritage and instinct. It had proclaimed the fact that "in these Churches we have been able to experience the healing and salvation of the Spirit *now* and not only in the afterlife".[43] In that study, however, in comparison to *The Kairos Document*, Archbishop Ngada and his colleagues had only tentatively begun to explore the political dimensions of their beliefs. They proclaimed that they and their church members knew what it meant to be oppressed, and that they also knew that "God does not approve of this evil and that racial discrimination and oppression is rejected by the Bible".[44] The seed of insight was already there; the full flowering was to be made manifest a year later in the ecumenical company of the Kairos theologians. Here, yet again, an African Christian understanding of evil was being widened and deepened in a cumulative fashion. This process was intensified when a group of more than 130 "concerned evangelicals", including those from the charismatic and pentecostal Churches, published a critique of their own theology and practice. As evangelicals they emphasized the problem of sin, but they denounced the bias in many of the sermons of their fellow evangelicals, and they denounced "the sin that has led us to this war . . . racism . . . classism and sexism . . . the sins of white South Africa". They eschewed their normal respect for law and order, for in South Africa this means

> that the oppressed and exploited masses of South Africa must orderly and peacefully submit to their oppressors and exploitors [sic].
> This to us is the Law of Satan and the Order of Hell.
> This, in the name of Jesus, we must resist![45]

The influence and implications of *The Kairos Document* will undoubtedly be very considerable. In South Africa, the defections of leading academics at Stellenbosch University, the intellectual matrix of Afrikaner nationalism and one of the strongholds of the conscience of the Afrikaner churches, may in part be attributed to its impact. Outside South Africa, its message is being carefully considered. It has been widely publicized by several official development agencies of the Catholic Church. Its analysis has been taken up and developed by other Third World theologians.[46] The Council of Churches in the Netherlands and the Evangelisches Missionswerk in West Germany have published warm statements of support. The latter is particularly significant for our theme. Having wholeheartedly expressed their desire to join with the Kairos theologians in resistance to "the inhuman system of apartheid", the Evangelisches Missionswerk response goes on to reflect further on some of the questions raised by the document. They appreciate the use of "apocalyptic categories like the 'anti-Christ' and the 'struggle between God and the Devil' to describe the situation" in South Africa. They agree that for two millenia, at times of extreme danger, Christians have turned to the Book of Revelation. "Apocalyptic language is the expression of the congregation in distress." Such language can, however, lead to dangerous simplifications. All statements from the adversary, threats as well as offers to negotiate, are reduced "to *one* single danger, which can no longer be addressed rationally". The use of apocalyptic images can lead to hatred and revenge. Similarly, it may lead to a triumphalist appropriation of

God's justice, of using God for one's own purposes. "There have been bad examples in our history," say these Germans, "of the use of the phrase 'God with us'. . . . Therefore we want to be reminded that God is never at our disposal. . . . Immanuel is the crucified one and not the God appropriated by the victorious".[47]

Thus around the symbol of Satan, some fundamental new developments have been occurring in African cosmologies and ethical insights. The dangers of becoming obsessively preoccupied with Satanic machinations or the plots of sorcerers are engrained in the historical experience of Europe, America and Africa. In a Christianized context, the dangers of any form of witch-hunt increase menacingly, it has been suggested by a student of Scotland, when peasant beliefs in witches are joined to an "active belief in the Devil among the educated".[48] Yet, real and terrible as these dangers undoubtedly are, they should not obscure the possibilities of a massive development in African concepts of evil. Faced with this new symbol of radical evil, Christians in Africa can see evil both in the hatreds and selfishness which tear apart small communities and in the structural exploitation which distorts so much of human activity in the contemporary world. And against the symbol of evil they can set the message of the Kingdom of God.

One should remember, however, that Christianity insists on the distinction between suffering and sin or radical evil. In a discussion of the mystery of death and suffering, one of the great Christian observers of Africa, Monica Wilson, reminded us that "evil [in the sense of suffering] accepted was the supreme revelation of good".[49]

At first sight this distinction, together with the willing acceptance of suffering, seems radically opposed to the values of most African cosmologies. The Cross challenges most human philosophies be they Greek, Roman or African. Confronted with disease and death, Africans, like most human beings, were generally concerned with preventing these afflictions. They sought an uncompromising conquest of evil. Mary Douglas has, however, suggested that this by no means exhausts African responses to the mystery of evil. In the pangolin cult of the Lele, the power for good is released by the death which the pangolin seems to accept deliberately. Similarly the sacrificial death of a Dinka spearmaster is perhaps not so fundamentally different from the welcome given to Sister Death by St Francis. Both correct the delusion that death and suffering are not an integral part of nature.[50] On an even wider front, Matthew Schoffeleers has pointed out that in certain respects the role of diviners or ritual-experts in some African societies can be seen as prefiguring that of Christ. In particular, this is the case, he argues, in the Malawian cult whose titular deity, Mbona, originally a gifted rainmaker, was put to death by the local ruler. But this happened, so the tradition runs, only after Mbona himself had told his slayers how to accomplish their task. This image of the sacrificed and slain diviner, Schoffeleers suggests, does not refer to the elimination of proximate causes of witchcraft, nor does it lead to the pursuit and identification of witches. Rather it proclaims "the elimination of all remote causes of witchcraft; in other words, everything in the social fabric that makes for greed, jealousy, lust for power and hostility. This, to become reality, would of necessity involve a radical transformation of society . . .". Here then the diviner becomes a prophet evoking "a vision of society in its ideal state".[51] The message of the Cross and of the Resurrection are no more alien to Africa than to any other part of the world.

Notes

INTRODUCTION TO PART ONE

1. J.W. Fernandez, *Bwiti: an Ethnography of the Religious Imagination in Africa*, Princeton, 1982.
2. Quoted in E. Stock, *History of the Church Missionary Society*, London, 1899, vol. I, p. 19.
3. J.C. Miller, *Kings and Kinsmen*, Oxford, Clarendon Press, 1976.
4. See, for example, the description of the Ke ritual in Bernard Maillard, *Pouvoir et Religion: Les structures socio-religieuses de la chefferie de Bandjoun* (Cameroun), Berne, Peter Lang, 1984.
5. Miller, *Kings and Kinsmen*, p. 166.

CHAPTER 1

1. This is the form given in the only document in Portuguese which mentions him. Archives of Propaganda Fide, Rome, Scritture riferite nei Congressi, Series Africa, Angola, Congo, etc. (hereafter SC Africa), 1, fo. 486, affidavit signed by Gaspar da Costa de Mezquita, Lisbon, 15 Feb. 1681. In the Italian documents, Mendouça is rendered Mendoza.
2. C.R. Boxer, *The Church Militant and Iberian Expansion, 1440–1770*, Baltimore, 1978, pp. 32–6.
3. J.F. Maxwell, *Slavery and the Catholic Church*, Chichester, 1975, pp. 67–8.
4. Boxer, *Church Militant*, p. 35.
5. Archives of Propaganda Fide, Scritture originale riferite nelle Congregazioni generali (hereafter SOCG), 490, fo. 140, undated petition.
6. SC Africa, 1, fo. 487. This Italian version (the original is missing) of an affidavit signed by Giacinto Rogio Monzon, Madrid, 23 Sept. 1682, states that Lourenço was "moreno naturale del Brasile" [a dark-coloured native of Brazil]. The affidavit signed by Gaspar da Costa (fo. 486) states that he was "homen pardo e natural deste Reino de Portugal" [a Mulatto and native of this kingdom of Portugal – which, of course, included Brazil].
7. SOCG, 250, fos. 439–40, Luis de Pistoia to prefect, 18 July 1665.

8. SC Africa, 1, fo. 486.

9. Ibid., fo. 487, Monzon's affidavit, 23 Sept. 1682.

10. J. Bossy, *Christianity in the West, 1400–1700*, Oxford, 1985, p. 58.

11. A.J.R. Russell-Wood, "Black and Mulatto Brotherhoods in Colonial Brazil: A Study in Collective Behavior", *Hispanic Amer. Hist. Rev.*, 54 (1974), 567–602. See also A.J.R. Russell-Wood, *The Black Man in Slavery and Freedom in Colonial Brazil*, London, 1982.

12. Russell-Wood, "Black and Mulatto Brotherhoods in Colonial Brazil", pp. 597–9.

13. Giovanni Antonio Cavazzi de Montecuccolo, *Istorica descrizione de' tre regni: Congo, Matamba et Angola*, Bologna, 1687, pp. 342–4, 493. See below, p. 45.

14. SOCG, 250, fo. 248, petition dated 29 June 1658.

15. A.J.R. Russell-Wood, *Fidalgos and Philanthropists: The Santa Casa da Misericordia of Bahia, 1550–1755*, London, 1968, p. 142.

16. A.C. de C.M. Saunders, *A Social History of Black Slaves and Freedmen in Portugal, 1441–1555*, Cambridge, 1982, pp. 150–6.

17. A. Brasio, *Os pretos em Portugal*, Lisbon, 1944, pp. 87–90. When Fra Girolamo Merolla da Sorrento arrived at Lisbon in November 1682 on his way to the Congo, he was befriended by a Black from Kongo who, Merolla claimed, said that he merely wished to repay "the obligation which we Kongolese owe to the Italian Capuchins": Girolamo Merolla da Sorrento, *Breve, e succinta relatione del viaggio nel regno di Congo*, Naples, 1692, p. 16.

18. SOCG, 490, fo. 140, undated petition. Compare also the statement by the Lisbon notary that Lourenço was "procurador bastante de todos os homems pardos" [competent procurator of all the Mulattos]: SC Africa, 1, fo. 486.

19. Archives of Propaganda Fide, Scritture riferite nei Congressi, Series America Meridionale, 1, fo. 309, affidavit of Francisco da Foncequa, Bahia, 2 July 1686.

20. SC Africa, 1, fo. 487, Monzon's affidavit, 23 Sept. 1682.

21. A. Rumeu de Armas, *Historia de la prevision social en España: cofradias, gremios, hermandades, montepios*, Madrid, 1944, pp. 272–4.

22. SC Africa, 1, fo. 486.

23. Ibid., fo. 490.

24. G. Botero, *Relationi universali*, Venice, 1640 edn., p. 557. This is the only reference in Part IV which could possibly have given rise to Lourenço's note. For a discussion of Paul III's bull *Sublimis Deus* of 2 June 1537, see Maxwell, *Slavery and the Catholic Church*, pp. 68–70.

25. The last six lines of the petition were evidently added by a second hand (SOCG, 490, fo. 140^v) and the wording of the petition suggests the hand of someone practised in curial correspondence.

26. Saunders, *Black Slaves and Freedmen in Portugal*, p. 268.

27. SOCG, 490, fos. 140^{r-v}, undated petition.

28. Boxer, *Church Militant*, p. 33.

29. For example, those which resulted in the letter of Cardinal Barberini of 6 Oct. 1660, referred to by Cavazzi, *Istorica descrizione de' tre regni*,

pp. 690–1.

30. SOCG, 490, fos. 136ᵛ–137ᵛ, summary of Archbishop Cibo's statement. See also notes based on his interview with the Spanish and Portuguese missionaries (fos. 138ʳ⁻ᵛ).

31. Archives of Propaganda Fide, Lettere della S. Congregazione (hereafter Lettere), 73, fos. 9ᵛ–10, Cibo to Millini, 6 Mar. 1684; fos. 10ᵛ–11ᵛ, letter in similar terms to nuncio in Lisbon.

32. The actual impact of this letter in Kongo itself was disastrously different from that intended by the cardinals and Archbishop Cibo: see below, Chapter 2.

33. Born into a prosperous family in the province of Brescia, Fra Giambattista had entered the University of Padua to study law. While a student there, he became aware of a religious vocation and was accepted into the Capuchin novitiate in 1641. He became "one of the most learned members who then adorned the Capuchin order". Valdemiro da Bergamo, I conventi ed i Cappuccini Bresciani, Milan, 1891, p. 165.

34. The MS entitled "Le Giornate Apostoliche ... dal P.F. Giovanni Belotti da Romano" is held in the General Archives of the Capuchins. It is described in T. Filesi and Isidoro de Villapadierna, La "Missio Antiqua" dei Cappuccini nel Congo (1645–1835), Rome, 1978, pp. 222–3. The account of Fra Giovanni's visit to Rome is on fos. 786–811. I am most grateful to Father Isidoro for showing me this account and for innumerable other acts of kindness and guidance.

35. Valdemiro da Bergamo, Conventi ed i Cappuccini Bresciani, p. 168.

36. Archives of Propaganda Fide, Acta 53, fos. 112–16, n. 34, 31 May 1683. See also J.M. Lenhart, "Capuchin Champions of Negro Emancipation in Cuba, 1681–1685", Franciscan Studies, 6 (1946), 195–217.

37. J.T. López Garcia, Dos defensores de los esclavos negros en el siglo xvii, Maracaibo and Caracas, 1982, p. 192. This book contains the defences written by the two Capuchins.

38. SOCG, 492, fos. 196ʳ⁻ᵛ, memorandum submitted by Joannes Baptista a Sabbio.

39. For example, the brief of 7 Oct. 1462: see Maxwell, Slavery and the Catholic Church, pp. 51–6.

40. Lettere, 74, fo. 97ᵛ, Cibo to Piazza, 12 Mar. 1685.

41. J. Metzler, "Controversia tra Propaganda e S. Uffizio circa una commissione teologica 1622–1658", Annales Pont. Universitas Urbanianae (1968–9), 47–62.

42. Lettere, 75, fos. 20ʳ⁻ᵛ, Cibo to the bishop of Angola, etc. The letters are undated. Probably they were sent on 26 Mar. 1686, as were the previous letters in this file. The letter immediately following them is dated 26 Apr. 1686. The cardinals in the General Congregation held on 26 Mar. 1686, after the decisions of the Holy Office had been received, considered a further request from "Lorenzo de Silva de Mendoza, a humble petitioner, [who] having come to Rome for important affairs concerning the Blacks, and having consumed what he had in an illness, and on account of his long stay in Rome", humbly requested the cardinals to grant him "some charitable subsidy to enable him to return

to his country in the Indies". Sadly one must report that this request was merely noted by the cardinals. SOCG, 495a, fos. 392–393^v.

43. Probably this is a reference to the briefs of Nicholas V of 1452 and 1454: see Maxwell, *Slavery and the Catholic Church*, p. 53.

44. SOCG, 495a, fo. 58. At the head of the undated petition a clerk has written "Seconda reclamazione a N^{ro} Sig^e et alla Sta Mre Chiesa reclamando Giustizia" (second complaint to the holy father and to holy mother church demanding justice).

45. SOCG, 495a, fo. 62, summary of the secretary's statement.

46. The Capuchins' propositions and the reply of the Holy Office are to be found in *Collectanea S. Congregationis de Propaganda Fide seu decreta instructiones rescripta pro apostolicis missionibus*, I Rome, 1907, item 230. Cardinal J.J. Hamer, O.P., when secretary of the Doctrinal Congregation, informed me by letter dated 16 Dec. 1981 that the Archives of the Congregation (formerly the Holy Office) "do not evidence any minutes or other notes" concerning their decisions of 20 Mar. 1686.

47. Lettere, 75, fos. 20^{r-v}. See n. 42 above with regard to the date of these letters.

48. SOCG, 495a, fos. 56–57^v, letters from nuncios to Cardinal Altieri, dated 20 Apr. 1684, 1 May 1684.

49. I.A. Wright, "The Coymans Asiento, 1685–1689", *Bijdragen voor Vaderlandsche Geschiedenis en Oudheidkunde*, 6 (1924), 23–62.

50. L. von Pastor, *History of the Popes*, Vol. XXXII, English trans., London, 1940, p. 3.

51. SOCG, 490, fos. 141^{r-v}, undated memorandum headed "Instructions for Mgr Cybo". Similar arguments in defence of the slave trade were advanced by the Jesuit António Vieira: see Boxer, *Church Militant*, p. 35.

52. T. Filesi, "L'epilogo della 'Missio Antiqua' dei Cappuccini nel regno del Congo (1800–1835)", *Euntes Docete*, 23 (1970), 434–5. See also G. Saccardo, "La schiavitu e i Cappuccini", *L'Italia Francescana*, 53 (1978), 75–113, reprinted in G. Saccardo, *Congo e Angola con la storia dell' antica missione dei Cappuccini*, 3 vols. Venice, 1983, Vol. III, pp. 263–305.

CHAPTER 2

1. T. Filesi and Isidoro de Villapadierna, *La "Missio Antiqua" dei Cappuccini nel Congo*, Rome, 1978.

2. Girolamo Merolla da Sorrento, *Breve, e succinta relatione del Viaggio nel regno del Congo nell' Africa meridionale*, Naples, 1692, p. 202.

3. A. and J. Churchill, *A Collection of Voyages and Travels*, Vol. I, London, 1704, p. 702.

4. A.F. Prévost, *Histoire générale des voyages*, Vol. IV, Paris, 1747, p. 539.

5. D. Muriel (pseud. C. Morelli), *Fasti Novi Orbis*, Venice, 1776, p. 467.

6. J. Margraf, *Kirch und Sklaverei*, Tübingen, 1865, p. 192.

7. L. von Pastor, *Geschichte der Päpste*, Vol. XIV, 2, Freiburg, 1930, p. 1001.

8. Archives of Propaganda Fide (APF). Lettere, 73, f. 8v–9.

9. Ibid.

10. Filesi and Isidoro de Villapadierna, *"Missio Antiqua"*, p. 223.

11. L. Jadin, "Andrea da Pavia au Congo, à Lisbonne, à Madère. Journal d'un missionaire, capucin, 1685–1702", *Bull. Inst. hist. belge de Rome*, 41 (1970), 382, n. 2.

12. L. Jadin, "Rivalités Luso-néerlandaises au Sohio, Congo, 1600–1675", *Bull. Inst. hist. belge de Rome*, 37 (1966), 160–1; and see below, p. 38.

13. Ibid., p. 287–8.

14. APF. Scritture riferite nei Congressi (SC). Africa, Angola I, f. 573v. Giuseppe Maria da Busseto to Cardinals, 4 April 1685. The fact that Fra Girolamo repeats verbatim in his book Fra Giuseppe Maria's phrase concerning Barbados (Merolla, *Breve, e succinta relatione*, p. 203) strongly supports the suggestion that his interpretation of Cibo's letter was moulded by his superior.

15. APF. SC. Africa, Angola II, f. 92. Giuseppe Maria da Busseto to Cardinals, 8 Mar. 1687.

16. Jadin, "Rivalités", p. 201.

17. Ibid., p. 194.

18. Jadin, "Andrea da Pavia", p. 387.

19. Merolla, *Breve, e succinta relatione*, p. 203–30.

20. Antonio Zucchelli da Gradisca, *Relazioni del viaggio, e Missione di Congo nell' Etiopia Inferiore Occidentale*, Venice, 1712, pp. 160–9.

21. APF. SC. Africa, Angola II, f. 571. Girolamo da Sorrento to Secretary, 3 Apr. 1692.

CHAPTER 3

1. The research on which this chapter is in part based was undertaken with the help of an award from the British Academy. I am most grateful to Fathers Joseph Metzler OMI and Isidoro de Villapadierna OFM Cap., then archivists respectively of Propaganda Fide and the Capuchin Generalate, for their advice and many acts of kindness. It was first published in *Africa* 53 (3), 1983 and I am greatly indebted to its editor, Professor J.D.Y. Peel, for his comments, suggestions and criticism.

2. G. Balandier, *Daily life in the Kingdom of Kongo from the Sixteenth to the Eighteenth Century* (Eng. trans.), London, 1968, pp. 254–5.

3. Archives of Propaganda Fide, Scritture originale riferite nelle Congregazioni generali (SOCG) 514, f.471, "Compendiosa relatione . . . data da me F. Andrea da Pavia" considered on 6 Apr. 1693.

4. Giovanni Antonio Cavazzi de Montecuccolo, *Istorica descrizione de' tre regni: Congo, Matamba et Angola*, Bologna, 1687, p. 4.

5. J.K. Thornton, *The Kingdom of Kongo: Civil War and Transition, 1641–1718*, Madison, 1983, p. 12.

6. A. Hilton, *The Kingdom of Kongo*, Oxford, 1985, pp. 113–15.

7. O. Dapper, *Beschreibung von Africa* (German trans.), Amsterdam, 1670, pp. 565–6; Thornton, *Kingdom*, pp. 54–5.

8. Thornton, *Kingdom*, p. 80.

9. Dapper, *Beschreibung*, pp. 561–2.

10. SC Africa I, f.573v, Giuseppe Maria da Busseto to Prefect, 4 Apr. 1685.

11. Girolamo Merolla da Sorrento, *Breve, e succinta relatione del viaggio nel Regno di Congo*, Naples, 1692, pp. 154, 236–48.

12. W. MacGaffey, *Custom and Government in the Lower Congo*, Berkeley, CA, 1970, p. 263.

13. Hilton, *Kingdom*, pp. 155–6.

14. Cavazzi, *Istorica descrizione*, pp. 123, 856.

15. L. Jadin, "Le clergé séculier et les Capucins du Congo et d'Angola aux xvie et xviie siècles", *Bulletin de l'Institute historique belge de Rome*, 36 (1964), 185–483.

16. L. Jadin, "Rivalités luso-néerlandaises au Sohio, Congo 1600–1675", *Bull. Inst. hist. belge de Rome*, 37 (1966), 137–360.

17. Hilton, *Kingdom*, pp. 184–190.

18. SC Africa I, f.365–6, Nuncio to Prefect, Lisbon, 3 May 1677.

19. SC Africa I, f.573v, Giuseppe Maria da Busseto to Prefect, 4 Apr. 1685.

20. I refer not so much to the well-known abilities of Joseph de Paris, the "Grey Eminence", but to the skills and achievements of other Capuchins such as Innocenzo da Caltagirone, Marco d'Aviano and Giacinto da Casale Monferrato. See Mariano d'Alatri (ed.), *Santi e Santità nell' Ordine Cappuccino* Vol. I, Rome, 1980.

21. L. Jadin, "Andrea da Pavia au Congo, à Lisbonne, à Madère. Journal d'un missionaire capucin, 1685–1702", *Bull. Inst. hist. belge de Rome*, 41 (1970), 387–9.

22. Hilton, *Kingdom*, pp. 192–8.

23. Merolla, *Relatione*, pp. 169–75.

24. Ibid., pp. 156–8; Jadin, "Andrea da Pavia", pp. 448–52.

25. J. Cuvelier, *Relations sur le Congo du Père Laurent de Lucques (1700–1717)*, Brussels, 1953, p. 58.

26. Merolla, *Relatione*, p. 168.

27. SC Africa III, f.298v, Antonio Barreto de Silva to Prefect, Sonho, 17 Jan. 1702.

28. W. MacGaffey, "The Religious Commissions of the Bakongo" *Man* (N.S.), 5 (1) (1970), 30.

29. Merolla, *Relatione*, p. 153.

30. Ibid., p. 119; Jadin, "Andrea da Pavia", p. 457.

31. Merolla, *Relatione*, p. 156.

32. Dapper, *Beschreibung*, p. 544.

33. Cavazzi, *Istorica descrizione*, pp. 45, 342–3.

34. C. Piazza, *La Missione del Soyo (1713–1716) nella relazione inedita di Giuseppe da Modena OFM Cap.*, Rome, 1973, pp. 54–6; Buenaventura de Carrocera, "Dos relaciones inéditas sobre la Mision Capuchina del Congo", *Collectanea Franciscana*, 16–7 (1946–7), 123–4.

35. Cavazzi, *Istorica descrizione*, pp. 45, 342–3.

36. SOCG 250, f.428v, Crisostomo da Genova's report, 10 Jan. 1665, referring to conditions prior to his departure from Angola in July 1663.

37. Jadin, "Rivalités", p. 290.

38. Antonio Zucchelli da Gradisca, *Relazioni del viaggio, e Missione di Congo nell' Etiopia Inferiore Occidentale*, Venice, 1712, p. 138.
39. Ibid.
40. Ibid., pp. 141–2.
41. Cavazzi, *Istorica descrizione*, pp. 45, 346–7.
42. Merolla, *Relatione*, pp. 227–34.
43. Ibid., p. 149.
44. SC Africa II, f.314–15 and 573v, Angelo Francesco da Milano to Prefect, Luanda, 4 Mar. 1690 and 15 Apr. 1692.
45. O. Chadwick, *The Popes and European Revolution*, Oxford, 1981, p. 149.
46. Merolla, *Relatione*, p. 106.
47. SOCG 514, f.471v, "Compendiosa relatione".
48. Merolla, *Relatione*, p. 399.
49. Ibid., p. 105.
50. Cavazzi, *Istorica descrizione*, pp. 123, 856.
51. Merolla, *Relatione*, p. 209.
52. Ibid., pp. 82–93.
53. Cuvelier, *Relations*, pp. 159, 171, 228.
54. J.M. Janzen and W. MacGaffey, *An Anthology of Kongo Religion*, Lawrence, KS, 1974, p. 16.
55. Ibid., pp. 4, 17.
56. Ibid., p. 3.
57. Jadin, "Rivalités", p. 292.
58. Giovanni Belotti da Romano, "Avvertimenti salutevoli . . .", f.287. MSS in Biblioteca Radini-Tedeschi, Bergamo.
59. Merolla, *Relatione*, p. 127.
60. Ibid., p. 135.
61. Jadin, "Andrea da Pavia", pp. 440–1.
62. SOCG 514, f.471v, "Compendiosa relatione . . ." 6 Apr. 1693.
63. SOCG 514, f.472–472v, Comments by Cardinal Carpegna.
64. Jadin, "Le clergé séculier", pp. 443–4.
65. See above, Chapter 2.
66. Merolla, *Relatione*, p. 220.
67. Zucchelli, *Relazione*, pp. 160–73.
68. SC Africa III, f.288–288v, Antonio Barreto de Silva to Cardinals of Propaganda Fide, Sonho, 4 Oct. 1701: ". . . ser eu Principe Catholico, e dezejar o acerto da minha salvação".
69. Cuvelier, *Relations*, pp. 180, 289.
70. Balandier, *Daily Life*, p. 225.
71. See above, p. 24.

INTRODUCTION TO PART TWO

1. Ngwabi Bhebe, *Christianity and Traditional Religion in Western Zimbabwe, 1859–1923*, London, Longman, 1979.
2. Leonard Thompson, *Survival in Two Worlds: Moshoeshoe of Lesotho 1786–1870*, Clarendon Press, Oxford, 1975, Ch.3.

3. Quoted in J.G. George, "Education and LMS Policy in their Cape and Bechuana Missions from 1800 to 1925, Ph.D., University of Kent, 1988, p. 249. See also A.J. Dachs, "Functional Aspects of Religious Conversion among the Sotho-Tswana", in M.F.C. Bourdillon (ed.) *Christianity South of the Zambezi*, Vol. II, Mambo Press, Gwelo, 1977, pp. 147–58.

4. Quoted in K.G. Molyneux, "African Christian Theology: a Study of Contrasting Theological Reflection in Zaire with Special Reference to Examples Selected from Roman Catholic, Kimbanguist and Protestant Church Bodies", Ph.D., University of London, 1988, p. 82.

5. Mgr Baunard, *Le Cardinal Lavigerie*, 2 vols, Paris, 1896, Vol. I, p. 157.

6. J. Ki-Zerbo, *Alfred Diban: premier chrétien de Haute-Volta*, Paris, 1983.

7. *Journal of Religion in Africa*, 18, (2) (1988), 198.

8. R. Horton, "African Conversion", *Africa*, 41 (2) (1971); 'On the Rationality of Conversion", *Africa*, 45 (3&4) (1975).

9. Horton, "African Conversion", p. 104; and "Rationality", p. 234.

10. See, however, the argument in S. Barrington-Ward, "The Centre Cannot Hold . . . Spirit Possession as Redefinition", in E. Fasholé-Luke et al. (eds) *Christianity in Independent Africa*, London, 1978.

11. Horton, "Rationality", p. 396.

12. Ibid.

13. J.S. Mbiti, *New Testament Eschatology in an African Background*, London 1971.

14. A notable exception is H. Häselbarth, *Die Auferstehung der Toten in Afrika*, Gütersloh, 1972.

15. E.E. Evans-Pritchard, *Nuer Religion*, Oxford, 1956, p. 154. See also M. Wilson, *Rituals of Kinship among the Nyakyusa*, London, 1957, p. 210.

16. Häselbarth, *Auferstehung der Toten*, pp. 39, 51, 65–6.

17. E.L. Mendonsa "The Journey of the Soul in Sisala Cosmology", *Journal of Religion in Africa*, 7 (1) (1975), 67–9.

18. J.M. Waliggo, "The Catholic Church in the Buddu Province of Buganda, 1879–1925", Ph.D., University of Cambridge, 1976, p. 36.

19. As a saintly Capuchin missionary to Angola observed in the seventeenth century, "Tale dotrina ben sminuzzata fà gran colpo ne rozzi petti di què Etiopi" – Giovanni Belotti da Romano, "Avvertimenti salutevoli . . .", MSS f.241, Biblioteca Radini-Tedeschi, Bergamo. Cf. Mbiti, *New Testament Eschatology*, p. 65, where he points out that the concept of Hell was an entirely novel introduction to the Akamba.

20. Mbiti, *New Testament Eschatology*, pp. 89–90.

21. e.g. B.R. Wilson, *Magic and the Millenium*, London, 1973. For a well argued case study, see Jane and Ian Linden, "John Chilembwe and the New Jerusalem", *Journal of African History*, 12 (4), (1971), 629–51.

22. Waliggo, "The Catholic Church", p. 36.

23. A. Colombaroli, *Nigrizia*, Oct. 1910.

24. Walker, 22. VI. 1888, quoted by Waliggo, "The Catholic Church", p. 54.

25. M. Wilson, *Communal Rituals of the Nyakyusa*, London, 1959, p. 187.
26. G. Shepperson, "The Place of John Chilembwe in Malawi Historiography", in B, Pachai (ed.) *The Early History of Malawi*, London, 1972, pp. 408, 420, for some examples.
27. "This new world [of the hereafter] has facilitated the discovery and experience of the *ego* . . . for it is a world dependent much on the individual decision, conception, Faith (or lack of it), work, and projection of the *ego*" – Mbiti, *New Testament Eschatology*, p. 90.
28. In the towns, for instance, important developments have been noted in traditional beliefs. The role of ancestors as personal guardians increases in importance and "a whole technique of prayer" has been evolved to meet the urban situation. See P. Mayer, *Townsmen or Tribesmen*, Cape Town, 1961, pp. 151–7.
29. For examples, see B.A. Pauw, *Christianity and Xhosa Tradition*, Cape Town, 1975, pp. 136–7.
30. A. Nitschke (ed.) *XVIe Congrès International des Sciences historiques*, III, Actes, Stuttgart, 1986, pp. 201–4. Although the report does not make this clear, this issue was in fact the most contested one in the session's debate.
31. J.D.Y. Peel, "Syncretism and Religious Change", *Comparative Studies in Society and History*, 10 (1968), 129.
32. R.I.J. Hackett, *Religion in Calabar: the Religious Life and History of a Nigerian Town*, Berlin, 1989, pp. 186–7.
33. M.L. Daneel, *Quest for Belonging*, Gweru, 1987, pp. 33, 253.
34. B.A. Oyetade, "Syncretism in Yoruba Christian Lyrics", seminar paper presented at School of Oriental and African Studies, London, 1987.
35. B. Kato, *Biblical Christianity in Africa*, Achimota, 1985, p. 26.
36. G.C. Oosthuizen, *Post-Christianity in Africa*, London, 1968, Vol. XI, p. 91. See also my review of his *Afro-Christian Religions*, Leiden, 1979, in *Bulletin SOAS*, 43 (1980), 415.
37. C.G. Baeta (ed.) *Christianity in Tropical Africa*, London, 1968, p. 148.
38. See above p. 62, and Molyneux, "African Christian Theology", p. 82.
39. J. Jonson, "Between the Scylla of Syncretism and the Charybdis of a Self-appointed Ghetto: Bengt Sundkler in Svensk Missionstidskrift during 25 Years", *Studia Missionalis Upsaliensia*, 39 (1984), 46.
40. B.G.M. Sundkler, *Bantu Prophets in South Africa*, London, 1948, p. 297.
41. A.I. Berglund, "Bengt Sundkler, Prophet among Prophets", *Studia Missionalia Upsaliensia*, 39 (1984), 25–7.
42. e.g., Sundkler, *Bantu Prophets*, 2nd edn, London, 1961, p. 302.
43. B. Sundkler, *Zulu Zion*, Uppsala, 1976, pp. 22, 305, 317.
44. M–L. Martin, *Kimbangu*, Oxford, 1975, pp. viii–xi.
45. Molyneux, "African Christian Theology", p. 157.
46. Quoted in O. Bimweny-Kweshi, *Discours théologique Negro-Africain: Problème des fondements*, Paris, 1981, p. 270.
47. S. Sykes, *The Identity of Christianity: Theologians and the Essence of Christianity from Schleiermacher to Barth*, London, 1984, pp. 254–7.
48. O. Chadwick, *From Bossuet to Newman*, 2nd edn, Cambridge, 1987,

pp. xix–xx.
49. A.D. Nock, *Conversion*, London, 1961 edn, pp. 7, 14.
50. See, for example, J. M. Waliggo, "The Religio-political Context of the Uganda Martyrs and its Significance", *African Christian Studies*, 2(1), (1986), 25–9.

CHAPTER 4

1. This essay was first published in the *Journal of Black Studies*, 13(1) September 1982. In revising it, I have incorporated large sections of two other articles: "The origins and Organisation of the Nineteenth-century Missionary Movement", *Tarikh*, 3(1), (1969), and "Christianity and Religious change in Africa", *African Affairs*, 77 (306), 1978.
2. This prediction was made by D.B. Barrett, "A.D. 2000: 350 Million Christians in Africa", *International Review of Mission*, 59 (1970). See also the comments by A.F. Walls, "Towards Understanding Africa's Place in Christian History" in J.S. Pobee (ed.) *Religion in a Pluralistic Society*, Leiden, 1976.
3. See, for example, the different interpretations concerning the case of Uganda in R. Oliver, *The Missionary Factor in East Africa*, London, 1952 and in R. Robinson and J. Gallagher, *Africa and the Victorians*, London, 1965.
4. C. Fyfe, *A History of Sierra Leone*, London, 1962; J. Peterson, *Province of Freedom: A History of Sierra Leone, 1787–1870*, London, 1969.
5. J.F.A. Ajayi, *Christian Missions in Nigeria, 1841–1891: the Making of a New Elite*, London, 1956; E.A. Ayandele, *The Missionary Impact on Modern Nigeria, 1842–1914*, London, 1966; G.O.M. Tasie, *Christian Missionary Enterprise in the Niger Delta, 1864–1918*, Leiden, 1978.
6. F.L. Bartels, *The Roots of Ghana Methodism*, Cambridge, 1965, N. Smith, *The Presbyterian Church of Ghana, 1835–1960*, Accra, 1966.
7. But see also the account of African pioneers in J. van Butselaar, *Africains, Missionnaires et Colonialistes: Les origines de l'Église Presbytérienne du Mozambique (Mission Suisse), 1880–1896*, Leiden, 1984.
8. R. Horton, "African Conversion", *Africa*, 41 (1971), 85–108; idem, "On the Rationality of Conversion", *Africa*, 45 (1975), 219–35, 373–99.
9. H.J. Fisher, "Conversion Reconsidered: Some Historical Aspects of Religious Conversion in Black Africa", *Africa*, 43 (1973), 27–40; idem, "The Juggernaut's Apologia: Conversion to Islam in Black Africa", *Africa*, 55 (1985), 153–73.
10. J. Vansina, "Les mouvements religieux Kuba (Kasai) à l'époque coloniale", *Études d'histoire africaine*, 2 (1971), 155–87.
11. T.O. Ranger, "The Mwana Lesa Movement of 1925", in T.O. Ranger, and J. Weller (eds) *Themes in the Christian History of Central Africa*, London, 1975.
12. H.F. Hinfelaar, "Religious Change among Bemba-speaking Women of Zambia", Ph.D., University of London, 1989; B.A. Pauw, *Christianity and Xhosa Tradition*, Cape Town, 1975. For a fuller discussion of the changing concepts of evil, see also Chapter 5, below.

13. H.W. Turner, *African Independent Church*, 2 vols, Oxford, 1967; B. Sundkler, *Zulu Zion and some Swazi Zionists*, Uppsala, 1976.

14. G.M. Haliburton, *The Prophet Harris*, London, 1971; S.S. Walker, *The Religious Revolution in the Ivory Coast: the Prophet Harris and the Harrist Church*, Chapel Hill, NC, 1983; M. Martin, *Kimbangu*, Oxford, 1975; W. Ustorf, *Afrikanische Initiative: Das aktive Leiden des Propheten Simon Kimbangu*, Frankfurt, 1975; W. MacGaffey, *Modern Kongo Prophets: Religion in a Plural Society*, Bloomington, IN, 1983.

15. A most helpful discussion of this whole question, especially as it relates to Africa, is to be found in A. Shorter, *Jesus and the Witchdoctor: an Approach to Healing and Wholeness*, London, 1985.

16. See above, pp. 67–9.

17. J. Janin, *Le Clergé Colonial de 1815 à 1850*, Toulouse, 1935; J. Metzler (ed.) *Sacrae Congregationis de Propaganda Fide Memoria Rerum, 1622–1972*, 3 vols, Rome, 1971–5.

18. S. Delacroix (ed.) *Histoire universelle des Missions Catholiques*, 4 vols, Paris, 1956–9, Vol. III, p. 43.

19. Quoted in E. Stock, *History of the Church Missionary Society*, London, 1899, Vol. I, p. 60.

20. R.N. Slade, *English-speaking Missions in the Congo Independent State (1878–1908)*, Brussels, 1959. See also J. Stengers in R. Oliver and G.N. Sanderson (eds) *The Cambridge History of Africa*, Cambridge, 1985, Vol. VI, pp. 315–27.

21. Stock, ibid., Vol. I, pp. 474–80.

22. Delacroix, ibid., Vol. III, p. 64. See also S. Beltrami, *L'Opera della Propagazione della Fede in Italia*, Florence, 1961.

23. R.S. Maloney, *Mission Directives of Pope Gregory XVI, (1831–1846): a Contribution to the History of the Catholic Mission Revival in the Nineteenth Century*, Rome, 1959. The young Angelo Roncalli (later John XXIII) was closely involved in these 1922 negotiations.

24. M.B. Storme, *Evangelisatiepogingen in de Binnenlanden van Afrika gedurende de XIXe eeuw*, Brussels, 1951.

25. A. Ross, *John Philip (1775–1851)*, Aberdeen, 1986.

26. K.J. King, *Pan-Africanism and Education*, London, 1971.

27. D. Lagergren, *Mission and State in the Congo*, Uppsala, 1970.

28. Some useful hints can be found in Jehan de Witte, *Monseigneur Augouard: sa vie*, Paris, 1924.

29. M.D. Markowitz, *Cross and Sword: the Political Role of Christian Missions in the Belgian Congo, 1908–1960*, Stanford, CA, 1972.

30. For examples, see *Les relations entre l'église et l'état au Zaïre*, Études africaines du CRISP, Brussels, 1972.

31. Ngindu Mushete, "Authenticity and Christianity in Zaïre", in E. Fashole-Luke et al. (eds) *Christianity in Independent Africa*, London, 1978.

32. R. Gray (ed.), *The Cambridge History of Africa*, Cambridge, 1975, Vol. IV, p. 1.

33. C. Fusero, *Antonio Vignato nell'Africa di ieri*, Bologna, 1970, pp. 127–8.

34. B. Garvey, "The Development of the White Fathers' Mission among the Bemba-speaking Peoples, 1891–1964", Ph.D., University of Lon-

don, 1974.

35. L. Sanneh, *Translating the Message: the Missionary Impact on Culture*, New York, 1989.

36. H.S. Dulp, quoted in T.M.B. Mapuranga, "The Emergence of Ekklesiyar Yan'uwa a Nigeria, an Historical Analysis, 1923–1977", Ph.D., University of London, 1980.

37. J. McCracken, *Politics and Christianity in Malawi 1875–1940*, Cambridge, 1971.

38. F.K. Ekechi, *Missionary Enterprise and Rivalry in Igboland 1857–1914*, London, 1971.

39. Sir Hugh Clifford quoted in *Education in Africa: a Study of West, South and Equatorial Africa* (Report of the Phelps-Stokes Commission prepared by T. Jesse Jones), New York and London, 1922, p. 175.

CHAPTER 5

1. B.G.M. Sundkler, *Bantu Prophets in South Africa*, London, 1948.

2. Quoted in G. Shepperson, "The Politics of African Church Separatist Movements in British Central Africa, 1892–1916', *Africa*, 24 (1954), 240.

3. See above, Chapter 1.

4. Quoted in D.J. Cook, "The Influence of Livingstonia Mission upon the Formation of Welfare Associations in Zambia, 1912–31', in T.O. Ranger and J. Weller (eds) *Themes in the Christian History of Central Africa*, London, 1975, p. 108.

5. Quoted in F. Macpherson, *Kenneth Kaunda of Zambia: the Times and the Man*, London, 1974, p. 70.

6. G. Verstraelen-Gilhuis, *From Dutch Mission Church to Reformed Church in Zambia*, Franeker, 1982, pp. 165–6.

7. Ibid., p. 171.

8. *Report of the Jerusalem Meeting of the International Missionary Council*, London, 1928, Vol. V, p. 163.

9. G. Wilson, *An Essay on the Economics of Detribalization in Northern Rhodesia*, Livingstone, 1941–2; R.J.B. Moore, *These African Copper Miners*, London, 1948.

10. A. Nolan, *Jesus Before Christianity*, London, 1977, pp. 140–1. In his *God in South Africa*, London, 1988, Nolan has powerfully developed this analysis, especially in Chapter 4.

11. M. Douglas, *Purity and Danger*, London, 1966.

12. M. Southwold, "Buddhism and Evil", in D. Parkin (ed.) *The Anthropology of Evil*, Oxford, 1985, pp. 130–2.

13. Quoted in R.G. Stuart, "Christianity and the Chewa: the Anglican Case, 1885–1950", Ph.D., University of London, 1974, pp. 230–2.

14. W. de Craemer, J. Vansina and R.C. Fox, "Religious Movements in Central Africa: a Theoretical Study", *Comparative Studies in Society and History*, 18 (1976), 458–75. For an earlier example see above p. 45.

15. S. Barrington-Ward, "'The Centre Cannot Hold . . .': Spirit Possession as Redefinition", in E. Fashole-Luke et al. (eds) *Christianity in Independent Africa*, London, 1978.

16. J. Comaroff, *Body of Power, Spirit of Resistance: the Culture and History of a South African People*, Chicago, 1985, pp. 176–201.

17. R. Gray, "Christianity", in A. D. Roberts (ed.) *The Cambridge History of Africa*, Vol. VII, 1986, pp. 168–9.

18. J.M. Janzen and W. MacGaffey, *An Anthology of Kongo Religion*, Lawrence, KS, 1974, p. 3.

19. L. Sanneh, *West African Christianity: the Religious Impact*, New York, 1983, pp. 243–8.

20. M. Weber, *The Sociology of Religion* (English trans.), London, 1966, edn, p. 38.

21. I owe to Dr H.J. Fisher the insights into the significance of the cumulative impact of the world religions in Africa; see, for example, H.J. Fisher, "The Juggernaut's Apologia: Conversion to Islam in Black Africa", *Africa*, 55 (1985), 158–62.

22. The first time Luke mentions the kingdom of God (Luke IV, 43) was after the first exorcisms at Capernaum, 'the preliminary skirmishes in the campaign to be waged . . . against the kingdom of Satan'. G.B. Caird, *The Gospel of St Luke*, Harmondsworth, 1963, p. 89.

23. S. Kaplan, *The Monastic Holy Man and the Christianization of Early Solomonic Ethiopia*, Wiesbaden, 1984, pp. 70–4.

24. W.H. Sangree, *Age Prayer and Politics in Tiriki, Kenya*, London, 1966, p. 164 (italics in original).

25. J.M. Janzen with W. Arkinstall, *The Quest for Therapy in Lower Zaire*, Berkeley, CA, 1978, pp. 97–8.

26. K.E. Fields, *Revival and Rebellion in Colonial Central Africa*, Princeton, NJ, 1985.

27. In earlier times the people of Kongo intimately connected the slave trade with the activities of witches. W. MacGaffey, *Modern Kongo Prophets: Religion in a Plural Society*, Bloomington IN, 1983, pp. 134–8. See also his *Religion and Society in Central Africa*, Chicago, 1986, especially Chapters 7 and 8.

28. T.O. Ranger, *The African Voice in Southern Rhodesia*, London, 1970, p. 206.

29. Fields, *Revival and Rebellion*, p. 140.

30. Ibid., p. 284.

31. Quoted in C. Perrings, "Consciousness, Conflict and Proletarianization: an Assessment of the 1935 Mineworkers' Strike of the Northern Rhodesian Copperbelt", *Journal of Southern African Studies*, 4 (1977), 50.

32. Quoted in Ranger, *African Voice*, p. 213.

33. I. Cunnison, "A Watchtower Assembly in Central Africa", *International Review of Missions*, 40 (1951); S. Cross, "Independent Churches and Independent States: Jehovah's Witnesses in East and Central Africa", in Fasholé-Luke, *Christianity in Independent Africa*, pp. 304–15.

34. E. Milingo, *The World in Between: Christian Healing and the Struggle for Spiritual Survival*, London, 1984, pp. 12–15.

35. Ibid., pp. 9 and 34–5.

36. Ibid., p. 37.

37. D. Shank, "A Prophet of Modern Times: the Thought of William

Wade Harris, West African Precursor of the Reign of Christ", Ph.D., University of Aberdeen, 1980.

38. C.D. Maire, "Dynamique Sociale des Mutations Religieuses: expansions des Protestantismes en Côte d'Ivoire", Méoire de diplôme, École Pratique des Hautes Études (VI), Paris, 1975, quoted by R. Hollinger-Janzen, "The Prophet Harris's Understanding of Evil", MA dissertation, University of London, 1986, p. 19. My discussion of Harris owes much to Hollinger-Janzen.

39. Hollinger-Janzen quoting reports by Caseley Hayford, Hartz and Benoit of Harris' words.

40. F.D. Muzorewa, "Through prayer to action: the Rukwadzano women of Rhodesia", in Ranger and Weller, *Themes*, pp. 257–8.

41. *The Kairos Document*, Braamfontein, 1985; reprinted in Third World Theology, series, Catholic Institute for International Relations, London, 1986, no. 10. Frank Chikane in W.H. Logan (ed.) *The Kairos Covenant*, New York, 1988, p. 45, has given a valuable insight into the process by which the document evolved. He reports: "we had a heavy argument about the word (devil), and the people in the townships said, "Ka si, Sotho ki Santani" (This system is a Satan). They were trying to express their idea in the language they use in the streets. They were saying, "This is a devil and we must deal with it".

42. Ibid., p. 26. Nolan, *God in South Africa* is an extended examination of the theology of the *Kairos Document* by one of its signatories.

43. *Speaking for Ourselves*, Institute of Contextual Theology, Braamfontein, 1984, p. 23.

44. Ibid., pp. 26–7.

45. *Evangelical Witness in South Africa*, Dobsonville, South Africa 1986, pp. 13–19. One of the principal signatories of this document was Frank Chikane, whose autobiography, *No Life of My Own*, London, 1988, is a vivid and detailed account of how this Pentecostal set out to reappropriate the Bible and apply it against a wider concept of evil and injustice.

46. *The Road to Damascus: Kairos and Conversion*, a document signed by Third World Christians and published by CIIR, Center of Concern and Christian Aid, London and Washington, 1989.

47. F.J. Verstraelen, "Responses to the Kairos Document", *Mission Studies*, 3(1), (1986), 71–2.

48. C. Larner, *Enemies of God. The Witch-hunt in Scotland*, Oxford, 1983, p. 193. For a warning of the danger in Africa, see A. Hastings, *African Catholicism: Essays in Discovery*, London, 1989, p. 149, for his remarks on some of Milingo's views. I am also greatly indebted to Mary Douglas for sharing with me her account of Catholic anti-sorcery movements among the Lele.

49. M. Wilson, *Religion and the Transformation of Society*, Cambridge, 1971, p. 142, quoting H.A. Williams.

50. Douglas, *Purity and Danger*, Ch.10.

51. M. Schoffeleers, "Folk Christology in Africa: the Dialectics of the Nganga Paradigm", *Journal of Religion in Africa*, 19(2), (1989), 157–83.

Index